FRIENDSHIP IS THE CROWN

THE SACRED QUEST TO BE GOD'S FRIEND

BY STEVE HARRISON

Friendship is the Crown: The Sacred Quest to be God's Friend

Ardor Media
P.O. Box 302
Brainerd, MN 56401

ISBN 979-8-9911792-9-4 (soft cover)
ISBN 979-8-9911792-8-7 (eBook)

First printing: 2025
Printed in the United States of America

Dedication

I would like to dedicate this book to my grandchildren. They represent a generation that God is preparing to shake the world. They have a unique calling grounded in Christ's faithfulness and sustained by His goodness. Walk, run, fly and hold on to the promise: "But they that wait upon the LORD shall renew their strength; they shall mount up with wings as eagles; they shall run, and not be weary; and they shall walk, and not faint" (Isaiah 40:31).

Table of Contents

Foreword

I've had the privilege of knowing Steve Harrison since the fervent days of the Jesus Movement in the seventies. Over the decades, I've observed his life, both from close proximity and from a distance, and what has always shone through is his unwavering pursuit of a profound truth: that the highest calling from God isn't simply to serve Him, but to be His friend.

In "Friendship is the Crown," Steve unpacks this eternal principle with wisdom and insight, reminding us of the precious bond that the enemy of our souls so desperately wants to steal. This book isn't just theory; it's the overflow of a life lived in the light of this divine friendship. I can think of no one more qualified than Steve to write about being a friend of God. He's truly a man after "God's own heart."

The personal stories and penetrating questions at the end of each chapter will challenge you to draw much closer to the Lord. I'm already looking forward to reading the book again and getting it into the hands of my friends. John 15:15 "No longer do I call you servants, for a servant does not know what his master is doing, but I have called you friends, for all things that I heard from my Father I have made known to you."

Peter W. Cawthon III
Missionary
Commission to Every Nation

Introduction

I remember my dad saying something profound a few years before he died: "It takes a lifetime to figure out what life is all about, and then you die." I believe he said it tongue-in-cheek, but there is some truth to it. I guess the best thing is to figure out life as early as possible, as this will allow you to get the most out of life.

As I have gotten older, I have discovered the value of simple things. I find myself getting rid of clutter in the garage and shed. I enjoy removing unnecessary files in my office. I am culling down my books to the essentials. Instead of attending to *things*, I now focus more on relationships. To me, this is living smarter not harder. Acknowledging that I am in the twilight of my years, I remember an admonition I once received from the Lord: "Christian maturity isn't measured by how smart or sophisticated you become but when the simple truths of the Gospel become more real."

Over the years, I have enjoyed reading my Bible. What started off as a Christian duty has grown to be one of the most inspiring parts of my day. I like to listen to the Bible while watching it on scrolling text with my wife, Martha. Now that I am retired, it has been easier to do this together. We get through the Bible at least once a year. I can't tell you how many times I've read it, but I've been a Christian for over fifty years.

There are so many aspects of the Bible that I enjoy, but I love to discover broader themes. These themes are interesting because they often reveal what is important to God. Friendship is one of those broader themes. It is a simple concept but a profound one. Jesus said if we abide in Him, we will bear much fruit (John 15:5). Nothing complicated about that. Abiding in Jesus bears fruit. It's a promise, a guarantee. I have been meditating on the subject of friendship for many years, so I thought it was time to get some of my thoughts down.

I'll never forget hearing a sermon years ago by Judge Lindsey, an old country preacher. The title of his message was "Palm Tree Christians." His sermon text was Psalm 92, which states, "The righteous will flourish like a palm tree, they will grow like a cedar of Lebanon; planted in the house of the LORD, they will flourish in the courts of our God. They will still bear fruit in old age, they will stay fresh and green" (v. 12-14).

He gave several points paralleling a mature Christian to a palm tree. The last point stuck with me the most. He said you can tell an old palm tree from the rest because "the older the palm, the sweeter the fruit." I like that a lot. If I abide in Christ, I will bear much fruit and as I get older, the fruit will become much sweeter. I want to be God's friend, plain and simple. I trust you do too.

Join me as we explore God's tender heart and His relentless pursuit of our friendship.

Chapter One
The Call to Friendship

"Friendship is the golden thread that ties the heart of all the world."
JOHN EVELYN[1]

A friend loves at all times. PROVERBS 17:17

SACRED FRIENDSHIP

Anticipation had reached a fever pitch. After a week of powerful, timely messages from men and women of God, it was now the final night of our annual conference at our national headquarters. David Wilkerson, founder of the Teen Challenge treatment centers, was the guest speaker; I knew in my heart the Lord had something to say to us through Brother Dave.

The title of his message was *The Lonely Jesus*. He explained a familiar type of prayer: going to God with a list of desires and needs we want God to do for us. There is nothing wrong with this type of prayer with God as it typically includes a list of good things for us and our family—things that a good God desires for His children. This part of our relationship with God is beautiful, except for one thing: generally, after we go through

---

[1] Goodreads, "John Evelyn," last modified April 14, 2025, https://www.goodreads.com/quotes/7960664-friendship-is-the-golden-thread-that-ties-the-heart-of.

1

our list, we get up and leave. In our minds, our job is done. Unfortunately, we often leave out a critical part. We rarely take the time to listen to God. We talk to Him about our needs but don't listen to Him about His desires and burdens. We don't allow Him to share His heart and don't take the time to consider His feelings.

David Wilkerson's message cut my heart. I was broken and humbled by my insensitivity to God's heart during my prayer times. I was determined to make some changes.

After the service, I gathered my personal belongings and prepared for the trip ahead—our team had been given a ministry assignment in Los Angeles to begin following the conference. Since the project was 1,500 miles from our ministry headquarters, we decided to leave immediately following the conference and drive through the night. Soon, we were heading west on Interstate 20 with hearts full of joy and gratefulness.

Late in the night, it was my turn to drive. A colleague and I discussed the conference, particularly *The Lonely Jesus* message. As we did, I suggested something a bit radical. I said, "We've been discussing the need to allow Jesus to share what is on His heart, but we are not doing it. Why don't we ask Him right now?" We then said a simple prayer inviting Him to do so. To my shock, the Lord spoke to us immediately and powerfully. It wasn't an audible voice, but it was so loud and clear that it had the same impact. He said, "I know you are working hard to be my servants, and I appreciate it. But there is something I want more than servants, **I want friends.**"

I mentioned this story in my first book, *Consuming Love*, because it was a significant event in my young Christian life. Fifty years have passed, and I now see friendship as a critical subject for every person. The Christian life hasn't always been easy, but I can't imagine it without knowing this aspect of God's heart.

REALIGNING PRIORITIES

I can confidently say that this word from the Lord has impacted me more than anything He has said in the fifty years since. It was simple but incredibly profound. I doubt I would be writing this book if it had not happened.

His revelation gave me a unique perspective on the Christian life—it is not what I do outwardly but who I am inwardly that God is most interested in. I no longer have to worry about wandering from the faith because I will never abandon a friendship I value above all others. I can be content in His arms, knowing He is content with holding me.

There was a time when I was part of a ministry called the Agape Force. It had formed during the Jesus Revolution in the 1970s. Revival was in the air, and we saw young people getting saved, healed, and delivered throughout the country. I was committed to this lifestyle and ministry, but there was a problem. Slowly, silently, and often subconsciously, I became obsessed with winning the approval of God and others. I was *doing the work of a Christian* more than *being a Christian*. I compared myself to others: "Am I matching others in Bible reading and prayer?" "Can I preach a better sermon or witness more effectively than my coworkers?" Without realizing my error, I had created a performance-based religion that would eventually burn me out.

I thought the key to pleasing God was *trying harder* instead of *loving more*.

But God, in His infinite grace and wisdom, interrupted my human efforts and worked to get me back on track. I realized if breaking me of my pride was important to Him, it needed to be important to me. At first glance, true friendship may seem like a relatively simple concept, but I believe it is comprehensive for many reasons. God uses many metaphors to explain Himself to us. Notably, He uses two key metaphors for our relationship with Him. One is of a Heavenly Father who leads us with parental affection and correction. The other is Jesus depicted as the Bridegroom and the Church as His bride. These are excellent metaphors but there are some unintended consequences.

THE UNCREATED RELATIONSHIP

Today, some people are living with scars from an abusive father. Perhaps their dad abandoned them at an early age. Maybe they were beaten or sexually abused. Often termed as "Betrayal Trauma," these deep emotional wounds are frequently the most difficult to heal. Broken trust inevitably produces a fractured relationship. Tragically, they can become a hinderance in trusting God as one's Heavenly Father.

Several years ago, there was a significant push in Christian circles to "know God more intimately." Many of us heard terms such as "Beloved," "Christ the Divine Bridegroom," and "intimacy with Christ" for the first time. The Song of Solomon was often used to share principles of intimacy. Some could relate, but those who were never married (not surprisingly) struggled to. Seeing God as a loving Father or a faithful Husband are but two ways we can understand our relationship with God. They are both beautiful, loving, and strong. As I mentioned, they are metaphors that God uses to reveal Himself to us. But what if there is another relationship that precedes father and husband? What if another type of relationship is most enduring? Which of all our relationships with God is the only uncreated relationship?

Before creation, the Father, Son, and Holy Spirit were in a relationship with one another. It wasn't a parent-and-child relationship because no one was created. It wasn't a marriage relationship either. It was a deep, abiding friendship.

Now, let me ask another question. What is the only eternal relationship? The Bible speaks of heaven as a place where there are no marriages. Consequently, no children will be born in heaven. There will be no need for the support and guidance of a mother and father. All there will be is friendships. Friendship with God—and each other—is a significant part of our eternal destiny. And I contend it is God's core relationship with all moral beings.

Fortunately, almost everyone has friends in their life. According to Melanie Dirks, PhD, "It is the first relationship in life that we get to freely choose."[2] The idea of friendship is universal and timeless. It involves the rich and poor, the educated and uneducated. It includes white-collar workers and those who are unemployed. Friendships are formed by churchgoers and members of gangs. I believe God hardwired us to experience the joy and comfort of friendship—we can't be human without it.

LORD OF THE RINGS

The Lord of the Rings is one of the most popular stories of all time, first told in book form and then in film. I admit it: I got

---

[2] Zara Abrams, "The science of why friendships keep us healthy," *American Psychological Association,* June 1, 2023, https://www.apa.org/monitor/2023/06/cover-story-science-friendship.

caught up in the drama and mystery when the films were first released. But what was the reason for the success of *The Lord of the Rings*? It is a story of enduring friendship amid tragedy and pain. I agree with self-proclaimed film critic Elise Sitzman,

> "At its core, *The Lord of the Rings* is about friendship. Ask almost anyone about the series, and chances are they'll say they wish they had a friend like Samwise Gamgee, or a leader like Aragorn, or a mentor like Gandalf . . . I could go on.
>
> It's a classic battle of good vs. evil with the good guys (and gals) coming together to form friendships that will last for centuries. At a time in the real world where tribalism and xenophobia are so rampant, it's refreshing to see different races and creeds coming together to fight the good fight. Even at the end of *Fellowship of the Ring*, when the fellowship is broken and all appears lost, the bonds of friendship help the characters press on. Sam refuses to let Frodo take the ring to Mt. Doom alone. And Aragorn, Legolas and Gimli band together to look for the hobbits and do their part to defeat Saruman."[3]

Who was the real hero of *The Lord of the Rings*? Even though the famed hobbit Frodo was the protagonist, and Aragorn returned as a king, I believe Samwise Gamgee was the ultimate friend and hero. Without his sacrifice and support, Mr. Frodo would never have completed his assumed task of destroying the ring on Mount Doom.

---

[3] Elise Sitzman "Friendship: The True Power of the Lord of the Rings Trilogy," *Film Perspective*, September 25, 2022, https://filmperspective. wordpress.com/2022/09/25/friendship-the-true-power-of-the-lord-of-the-rings-trilogy/.

Now, let me ask you an unusual question, "What is the Bible all about?" Is it about the nation of Israel? Is it about sinners being saved by grace? Is it about God's love or glory? Yes, that is all true, but I think it is primarily a story of a God who never gives up trying to become our friend. It's a story of a majestic King who rules wisely over His vast domain. And within His Kingdom, there lies a vulnerable race of beings who exist on a small planet that is cohabited by cruel and evil creatures bent on turning them to the dark side.

Despite their inferior intellect and moral failings, these weak human beings have secured a place in the King's heart. He seeks to aid them by winning their trust and guiding their efforts. Ultimately, they band together to destroy evil in the world. Afterward, the great King rewards them with eternal life in His royal Kingdom. Rather than a *fellowship of the ring*, it is the *fellowship of the cross*. Many would agree that it is the greatest story ever told, and it is a story of our being invited to live forever in the friendship of the Father, Son, and Holy Spirit that existed before Creation.

NOT GOOD TO BE ALONE

There were many things that God created and declared to be good. Moreover, after He made mankind, He proclaimed us to be *very good*. Unfortunately, something wasn't good, and God wanted to resolve it. "The LORD God said, 'It is not good for the man to be alone'" (Genesis 2:18).

Have you ever seen the reality TV show *Alone*? Ten contestants are put in a challenging environment without any access to the outside world or each other. The goal is to endure alone for as long as possible before "tapping out." The last person standing wins $500,000! Ironically, their most significant obstacle is probably the lack of human contact. This lack often overshadows their basic need for food and shelter. For most, their hearts give out before their bodies do. They can't stand to be separated from their loved ones any longer. This vividly illustrates a universal truth—God did not create us to live alone.

Studies have shown that people tend to live longer if they have companions. "People with no friends or poor-quality friendships are twice as likely to die prematurely, according to Holt-Lunstad's meta-analysis of more than 308,000 people—a risk factor even greater than the effects of smoking 20 cigarettes per day."[4] Furthermore, "loneliness increases the risk of early death as much as 26%."[5] And according to researchers, "What we know is that if we don't interact regularly, things go bad remarkably fast."[6]

We need others for protection. How are zebras protected from lions and cheetahs? It is not the zebra's speed, agility, or the power in its legs. It is the herd. If the zebra stays in the herd, no predator can focus on one zebra alone. Only when the zebra leaves the herd can it be easily identified, isolated, and killed.

The same is true with God's people. The enemy is much more effective if he can lure us away from Christian fellowship. I believe God has intentionally allowed this. The further we are from God and the Church, the more vulnerable we become. "Two are better than one, because they have a good return for their labor: If either of them falls down, one can help the other

---

[4] Zara Abrams, "The science of why friendships keep us healthy," *American Psychological Association*, June 1, 2023, https://www.apa.org/monitor/2023/06/cover-story-science-friendship.

[5] Ibid.

[6] Ibid.

up. But pity anyone who falls and has no one to help them up" (Ecclesiastes 4:9-10).

We also need the help of others to fulfill God's call for our lives. We can't bear the weight alone for very long. You see, the weight of our burden is not the concern but how many are helping us carry it. Moses couldn't fulfill God's command to destroy the Amalekites until he secured the help of Aaron and Hur (see Exodus 17:8-12). Jethro observed Moses' routine of judging Israel on his own and warned it was not sustainable. This resulted in a much-needed distribution and delegation of responsibilities to others under Moses' leadership (see Exodus 18:18-26). Later, in Israel's journey through the wilderness, Moses reached his limit in meeting the people's needs and was given the help of seventy capable and trustworthy men (see Numbers 11:16-17).

GOD'S FIRST FRIENDS

The Garden of Eden must have been incredibly beautiful. Can you imagine living in perfect harmony with nature and nature's God? The Bible said that Adam and Eve would meet daily with God in the cool of the day (see Genesis 3:8). God freely revealed Himself to them for friendship and direction. Even when they eventually sinned, the Bible tells us God personally made garments of animal skins for Adam and Eve and clothed them (see Genesis 3:21). They may have left the garden, but they never left God's heart.

Enoch was the great-great-great-great grandson of Adam. He lived to be 365 years old because of the extended lifespans of people at that time. Amazingly, Adam and Enoch coexisted for 308 years! Can you imagine Adam explaining to Enoch what it was once like in the Garden? The Bible tells us something special about Enoch: "Enoch walked faithfully with God; then he was no more, because God took him away" (Genesis 5:24). Notice the Scriptures tell us that Enoch "walked faithfully with God," not God walked faithfully with Enoch. I love how author Stony Kalango describes it: "A friend of God understands the ways of God because they walk with God. They understand how God works. They understand the deeds of God. They understand the heart of God. Why? Because they continually chase after God. They continually seek after God. They continually thirst for God. They continually desire God."[7]

As for Enoch's "being no more," most Bible teachers believe God supernaturally raptured Enoch to heaven, but I like to think he left long before that. Because of Enoch's friendship with God, there became less of him and more of God. Enoch became a reflection of God's character. I believe Enoch lost himself in God long before this earth lost him.

After the flood, the Bible mentions someone who was given the title of "God's friend." Abraham faced a series of spiritual challenges in his lifetime. As he passed them, he gained more favor with God. At one point, God decided to give him an incredible reward for his faithfulness: "I swear by myself, declares the LORD, that because you have done this and have not withheld your son, your only son, I will surely bless you and make your descendants as numerous as the stars in the sky and as the sand on the seashore. Your descendants will take possession of the cities of their enemies, and through your offspring all nations on earth will be blessed, because you have obeyed me" (Genesis 22:16-18). Wow, can you imagine becoming such a blessing to the world? This is what God can do for His friends.

---

[7] Stony Kalango, *Friend of God: Discover Diving Friendship as You Become One After God's Own Heart*, (2024), 81.

IS FRIENDSHIP WITH GOD NECESSARY?

Some people may question the need for having a friendship with God. They may surmise it is reserved for a few rare souls, and intellectual belief in God is sufficient for the rest of us. Is friendship with God essential for salvation? No. That is unless you are resisting His efforts to have you become His friend. Alexander MacLaren explains,

> "If not His friend, what are you? Have you only a far-off, bowing acquaintance with Him? Well, then, that is because you have neglected, if you have not spurned, His offered friendship. And, oh! how much you have lost! No human heart is a millionth part so sweet, and so capable of satisfying you as God's. All friendship here has its limits, its changes, its end. God's is boundless, immutable, eternal. All things are the friends of God's friend, and all things are arrayed against him who rejects God's friendship.
>
> I beseech you, let Him woo you to love Him, and yield your hearts to Him. If when we were 'enemies,' we were reconciled to God by the death of His Son, much more, being friends, all the fullness of His love and the sweetness of His heart will be poured upon us through the living Christ."[8]

An intimate connection with God gives us a greater sense of value and purpose: "Now this is eternal life: that they know you, the only true God, and Jesus Christ" (John 17:3). We see that we are not an accident or mistake in the world. We were created for a reason, and with God's help, we will see it fulfilled.

---

[8] Alexander MacLaren, "MacLaren's Expositions of Holy Scripture – James 2," *Bible Hub*, Accessed April, 15, 2025, https://biblehub.com/commentaries/maclaren/james/2.htm.

We can also experience God's feelings and thoughts about ourselves and others. I often say to God, "May all your dreams for me come true for your sake as well as mine."

As Christians, our friendship with God is unique among all the people in the world. Yes, He knows our name and so much more. The Bible states that His heart is moved with compassion for us. He is broken by those who reject Him, but He rejoices over those who seek to know Him. Oh, what a friend we have in Jesus!

ARE WE HIS FRIENDS?

The Bible states that Jesus was a friend of sinners. Doesn't that suggest that we are all God's friends already? Not necessarily. You see, God had a love for us long before we had a love for Him. Since Jesus is clearly a friend to us, the real question becomes, are we a friend to Him? Moses knew God was his friend, but he wanted to know if God considered him to be a friend. "If it is true that you look favorably on me, let me know your ways so I may understand you more fully and continue to enjoy your favor" (Exodus 33:13).

But doesn't the Bible say that Jesus will welcome His followers into heaven with the words, "Well done, good and faithful servant!" (Matthew 25:23)? Based on this, shouldn't we be content with just being His servant? I asked the Lord about this one time, and I sensed an immediate response in my spirit, "There are many more servants than friends. Every friend is a servant, but not every servant is a friend." Simply put, why would anyone settle for being a servant when friendship with God is offered?

I believe if we want to be friends with anyone, we must be intentional. My wife has said on a few occasions, "Don't tell me you love me. Show me you love me!" We can't be passive or hope it will happen. "A man who has friends must himself be friendly" (Proverbs 18:24, NKJV).

Do you want to be a friend of God? I believe most would say, "Yes."

Do you have a plan to do so? Most would say, "No."

FRIENDSHIP'S LEGACY

A few months ago, I happened on a podcast where Larry Randolph, a seventy-three-year-old Christian preacher, talked about his long ministry career. He was reflecting on his spiritual accomplishments and legacy. Then, he said something that strongly resonated in my spirit, "My goal at the end of this life, is not to be a great ministry but to be a friend of God." He went on to say, "If I am going to live for eternity, then I want to get as close to Jesus as I can get . . . Instead of me saying, 'Lord, help me,' I ask the Lord God, 'What's on your mind? What troubles you today? What hurts your heart today in the world? I want to be your friend. How can I help you with something?' Can I bear something instead of saying, 'God, me, me, me'?"[9]

God extends an open invitation for friendship to us all. I can look back at numerous times in my life when His tenderness and care were vividly displayed to me. I distinctly remember His healing touch when I was facing an extended sickness as a boy. I also remember being in the car with my mother as she drove at night through an intense rainstorm; after we prayed, the atmosphere immediately cleared. Many times, I've sensed His presence as an old hymn was sung, or a passage of Scripture was

---

[9] "Larry Randolph: A Global Awakening, Prophecy, and Coming Change," Iris Global, 2 hrs., 12 min., 11 sec., https://www.youtube.com/watch?v=sNCfeCvYoI8&t=9s&ab_channel=IrisGlobal.

read. Through the years, these and other events were deposited in my heart. Although I failed Him as a teenager, I have never left Him since, and that's been over fifty years! Below is a simple poem I wrote after coming back home to Him.

WHAT'S LIFE ALL ABOUT?

"What's life all about?" was the answer I sought.
"Who could lead me to find out?" was also my thought.

Everywhere I could see unrest seemed to rule;
Everyone seemed so selfish, so hateful, so cruel.

Then one day my questions were melted away
As one young man was prompted to say,

"There was an answer to all of Man's problems;
Man was to blame and from this base he must solve them.

From nature around and conscience within
A higher power is at work and to Him we give in.

And admit that we have, right from the start,
Lived for ourselves and broken His heart."

Well, I saw He was right and so I finally gave in.
God entered my life and cleansed me from sin.

I discovered His book and the meaning of prayer.
I saw His heartbreak and His longing to share.

Now I love this great God more than all the world's pleasures.
More than life, more than death, more than
earth's greatest treasures.

I vow to now serve Him till my task is complete.
Then I'll take all my labors and fall down at His feet.

REFLECTION AND DISCUSSION

Besides *The Lord of the Rings*, what other movie or book has featured friendship?

_____

_____

_____

What are the advantages of having friends in your life?

_____

_____

_____

Share the ways God has extended His love to you.

_____

_____

_____

Do you want to be a friend of God? If so, what are you willing to do?

_____

_____

_____

Chapter Two
Neighbors, Companions, and Friends

"Some people make enemies instead of friends because it is less trouble."
E.C. MCKENZIE[10]

There is a friend who sticks closer than a brother.
PROVERBS 18:24

FRIENDS FOR LIFE

In 1896, Thomas Edison, the great inventor of the electric bulb, was working on a car design when he learned that a young man in his company had created an experimental car. Edison met this young man, Henry Ford, at a company party in New York and was thoroughly impressed by his gasoline-powered car idea. Edison, who had been considering electricity as a power source, enthusiastically encouraged Ford, saying, "Young man, that's the thing! You have it! I think you are on to something! I encourage you to continue your pursuits!"

---

[10] Paul Lee Tan, *Encyclopedia of 7,700 Illustrations: Signs of the Times* (Assurance Publishers, 1979), 465.

Encouraged by the respected inventor, Henry Ford continued his work, eventually inventing a car that made him wealthy and, more importantly, changed an industry and the world.

On December 9, 1914, Edison's laboratory and factory were destroyed by fire. The damage was too extensive for insurance to cover. Before the ashes were cold, Henry Ford handed Edison a check for $750,000 with a note saying Edison could have more if needed.

Continuing their friendship, "in 1916, Ford relocated his home next to Edison's. When Edison was later confined to a wheelchair, Ford also got a wheelchair so they could race each other."[11]

Because of stories like this, I'm inspired to be a better friend to others. I see the beauty and value of such relationships but often overlook the process and pitfalls I may encounter in becoming a true friend.

A CULTURAL REALITY

The term *friend* is used in several ways in our culture, partly because it is such a positive concept. It can make the unpleasant more tolerable; it gives us renewed hope; it lightens our heavy loads. In your community, there is likely an auto mechanic who advertises *friendly* service. We know what that means: You'll be greeted with a smile and treated with respect. Their prices will be fair, and they'll provide excellent service. They'll offer friendliness as a professional courtesy.

---

[11] Gerry Moran, "Shedding Light on Friendship of Edison and Ford," *The Kilkenny Observer,* Accessed April 15, 2025, https://kilkennyobserver. ie/shedding-light-on-friendship-of-edison-and-ford/.

In social media, obtaining as many "friends" as possible is a common goal. In addition, we want them to "like" what we say and do. Their positive response gives us a sense of validation and significance.

There is an old adage: "A friend in need is a friend indeed." Friends are often found after a house fire, during an extended illness, or when a loved one struggles with addiction. If our country is threatened militarily, we seek friends (or allies) against a common foe. During times of peace, we trade with other countries through special business agreements. Friendship is a bright beacon of optimism in a world full of worry, suspicion, and darkness.

We can arrange friendships into three categories: neighbors or acquaintances, companions, and true friends. Interestingly, the journey to be a true friend often travels through the first two.

NEIGHBORS

Neighbors and acquaintances can be found in every aspect of your life; you often share at least one major area of interest. They may be in the same class in college. They may be a co-worker who shares common corporate values and goals. They might share a lawn or driveway, and you wave to each other when coming and going, and even talk a bit if you both happen to be raking your lawns. Or maybe you find a new acquaintance through a chance encounter when each of you is wearing a jersey of your favorite sports team, you smile and embrace an immediate kinship because you both want the same thing—a championship.

I believe most of our contacts on social media fall into this category. We may designate them "friends," but most are people we just know or even know of. We have some common points of connection but typically lack a deep emotional attachment to one another.

Neighbors were common in Bible times and were often mentioned in the New Testament. *Neighbor* comes from the Greek word *plēsiŏn*, meaning "close by" and was used in such passages as:

- "But he, wanting to justify himself, said to Jesus, 'And who is my neighbor?'" (Luke 10:29, NKJV)
- "Love does no harm to a neighbor. Therefore love is the fulfillment of the law." (Romans 13:10)
- "For the entire law is fulfilled in keeping this one command: 'Love your neighbor as yourself.'" (Galatians 5:14)

I remember going to a local coffee shop each Saturday with my wife, Martha. Over time, we got to know a particular waitress. (I will call her Stacy.) One day, I was shopping at a local store when I noticed Stacy. From about fifteen feet away, I said, "Hi, Stacy." She acknowledged me but quickly looked away. She seemed uncomfortable with the interaction, so I moved on. Later, we discovered she was pregnant, so we purchased some baby items for the newborn. She wasn't working the day we went to the coffee shop, so we gave the items to a fellow waitress, but we never heard from Stacy. She bused our table one time after but never mentioned anything about the gift. I had to accept that she didn't want to connect beyond taking our order.

Many people have this type of relationship with God. We want to be good neighbors— God has His business, and we have ours. We don't want to be a bother or infringe on God's business, and we expect the same from Him. We hope He is not loud after 10:00 p.m. and doesn't ask to borrow too many tools from us. Occasionally, we may talk about something of mutual interest.

While leading the Children of Israel in the wilderness, Moses encouraged them to get to know God better, but they often chose to remain distant: "All the people, experiencing the thunder and lightning, the trumpet blast and the smoking mountain, were afraid—they pulled back and stood at a distance. They said to Moses, 'You speak to us and we'll listen, but don't have God speak to us or we'll die.' Moses spoke to the people: 'Don't be afraid. God has come to test you and instill a deep and reverent awe within you so that you won't sin.' The people kept their distance while Moses approached the thick cloud where God was" (Exodus 20:18-21, MSG).

Many of Christ's followers believed in Him but kept themselves at arm's length: "Yet at the same time many even among the leaders believed in him. But because of the Pharisees they would not openly acknowledge their faith for fear they would be put out of the synagogue; for they loved human praise more than praise from God" (John 12:42-43).

Humanity, for an exceptionally long time, has relegated God to being a neighbor, or an acquaintance, hoping He'll be there for us when we are in need. But if we are to be true friends of God, doesn't He deserve so much more?

COMPANIONS

Now, let's move to a closer relationship called *companions*. These are the people who, at least at certain points in their lives, are on the same path as we are.

- A companion is someone you like to spend time with or enjoy being with.

- They can include neighbors, coworkers, roommates, and family members.
- They help us reach further on our paths—like marathon runners urging each other to keep running.
- A companion is often suited to helping us in our times of need since they truly understand our desires and our situation.[12]

When I think of companions in a biblical context, I picture the two disciples on the road to Emmaus. They were on a journey together. Suddenly, Jesus joined them, and for a while they travelled together. Their fellowship was sweet, and when Jesus left them, "they asked each other, 'Were not our hearts burning within us while he talked with us on the road and opened the Scriptures to us?'" (Luke 24:32).

The word *companion* comes from the Greek word *hĕtairŏs*, which means "a clansman or comrade." Interestingly, this word was only used by Jesus three times and only in the Gospel of Matthew.

- "But he answered one of them, 'I am not being unfair to you, friend. Didn't you agree to work for a denarius?'" (Matthew 20:13)
- "He asked, 'How did you get in here without wedding clothes, friend?' The man was speechless." (Matthew 22:12)
- "Jesus replied, 'Do what you came for, friend.' Then the men stepped forward, seized Jesus and arrested him." (Matthew 26:50)

---

[12] Ninjaapple, "The Difference Between a Friend and a Companion," *Hub Pages,* June 9, 2023, https://pairedlife.com/friendship/Know-Your-Relationships-Difference-Between-A-Friend-And-A-Companion.

I have had several companions, and you probably have too. Some are from my childhood and include schoolmates, neighbors, and cousins. Others were coworkers who fit perfectly in my world. Even more sat beside me in church or joined me in Bible studies.

These individuals have thoroughly enriched my life, but one thing I have noticed: the connection with my companions seemed to be only for a season. Inevitably, someone would move or change jobs, maybe a shared interest changed, or a disagreement. There could be a myriad of reasons but, eventually, our companionship ended.

This relational separation bothered me until I saw several instances of this in the Bible: God directed Abraham to leave his homeland. Jesus told His disciples that their family relationships would be affected if they followed Him. The Apostle Paul had ever-changing travelling companions like Barnabus, Silas, and Timothy. I began to see that in God's Kingdom, there are necessary endings in relationships that we eventually must accept.

FRIENDS

Friendship is still a coveted gold standard in our culture. It implies more common interests and a stronger emotional bond. Friendship often involves the following:

- a strong liking, trust, and a sense of closeness
- loyal support in good times and bad
- a source of comfort, encouragement, and a sense of belonging
- shared experiences, emotional support, and a deeper level of intimacy

Friendship comes from the Greek word *philŏs*, a term for friendship or affection. According to Webster's 1828 edition, friend is defined as: "One who is attached to another by affection; one who entertains for another sentiments of esteem, respect and affection, which lead him to desire his company, and to seek to promote his happiness and prosperity." I like that.

Friendship was a common concept in the New Testament and was used in familiar passages, such as:

- "But when you are invited, take the lowest place, so that when your host comes, he will say to you, 'Friend, move up to a better place.'" (Luke 14:10)
- "You will be betrayed even by parents, brothers and sisters, relatives and friends, and they will put some of you to death." (Luke 21:16)
- "The bride belongs to the bridegroom. The friend who attends the bridegroom waits and listens for him and is full of joy when he hears the bridegroom's voice." (John 3:29)

PETER'S STORY

Peter was one of Jesus' closest disciples, but one time, Jesus had to challenge Peter's commitment to their relationship: "'Truly I tell you,' Jesus answered, 'this very night, before the rooster crows, you will disown me three times.' But Peter declared, 'Even if I have to die with you, I will never disown you.' And all the other disciples said the same" (Matthew 26:34-35).

We all know that Peter failed this loyalty test, but all was not lost. When Jesus arose from the dead, He instructed the women to tell the disciples, particularly Peter, that He had risen (see Mark 16:1-7). It is apparent that Jesus was intentionally reaching out to Peter to restore their friendship, even though Peter had violated the trust that loyal friends possess. Jesus, who was the offended party, didn't hold any grievance or hurt.

Who should make the first move toward reconciliation if a husband has been unfaithful? The husband, of course.

Who made the first move when we turned from God? Amazingly, God did.

Jesus did so again on the Sea of Galilee:

> "When they had finished eating, Jesus said to Simon Peter, 'Simon son of John, do you love me more than these?' 'Yes, Lord,' he said, 'you know that I love you.' Jesus said, 'Feed my lambs.' Again Jesus said, 'Simon son of John, do you love me?' He answered, 'Yes, Lord, you know that I love you.' Jesus said, 'Take care of my sheep.' The third time he said to him, 'Simon son of John, do you love me?' Peter was hurt because Jesus asked him the third time, 'Do you love me?' He said, 'Lord, you know all things; you know that I love you.'" (John 21:15-17)

Three times Peter denied Jesus, and three times Jesus asked Peter the question, "Do you love me?" Note that Jesus approached Peter about their relationship first and then his ministry assignment second. This order is critical. Remember, God is looking for friends more than servants. This passage is also interesting because Jesus and Peter use two words for love in their exchange. It is commonly believed that Jesus was focusing on a higher form of love that involved choosing for the highest good of God and others (*agapaō*), while Peter was fixed on a close friendship (philĕō). But was that actually the case?

Upon deeper investigation, we discover that Jesus and the disciples often used both Greek words interchangeably. The

Apostle John refers to himself as "the disciple that Jesus loved" in four incidences (see John 13:23-25; 19:26-27; 20:2; and 21:7). However, in the first two, John uses the Greek word agapaō, but in the third incident, he uses the word philĕō. John wasn't confused in his description of Jesus' love for him. He recognized that both types of love could exist simultaneously. Also, in describing God's perfect love we have two interesting passages: "No, the Father himself loves (philĕō) you because you have loved (philĕō) me and have believed that I came from God" (John 16:27), and "For the Father loves (philĕō) the Son and shows him all he does" (John 5:20). The Father's love is certainly not inferior because He used philĕō instead of agapaō.

It would be a mistake to minimize a friendship with God by assuming that agapaō is a superior and more mature form of love than philĕō.

I believe it is equally important that we have a friendship with God, as choosing the highest glory of God and the good of others.

DO YOU KNOW HIM?

How do we measure Christian maturity? Is it the years we have been a Christian? A certain level of Bible knowledge? Age? Depth of Christian character? These are all good considerations, but let's see what the Bible has to say about this all-important question: "Thus says the LORD: 'Let not the wise man glory in his wisdom, Let not the mighty man glory in his might, Nor let the rich man glory in his riches; But let him who glories glory in this, That he understands and knows Me'" (Jeremiah 9:23-24, NKJV).

In the Old Testament, the word *know* was a Hebrew verb, *yâda*. In ancient Hebrew culture, knowledge was not merely intellectual but was deeply relational and experiential. The concept of "knowing" someone or something involved a holistic understanding that included emotional and spiritual dimensions. This was evident in the use of yâda to describe the intimate relationship between a husband and wife: "And Adam knew (yâda) Eve his wife, and she conceived and bore Cain" (Genesis 4:1). It was also used in describing the covenant relationship between God and His people: "You have searched me, LORD, and you know (yâda) me" (Psalm 139:1).

In the New Testament, we have a comparable situation. The Greek word for *know* is *ginōskō*. It is used by Mary when the angel announced that she would experience a supernatural conception. "Then Mary said to the angel, 'How can this be, since I do not know (ginōskō) a man?'" (Luke 1:34, NKJV). Once again, the same word of intimacy is used with God and His followers: "Now this is eternal life: that they know (ginōskō) you, the only true God, and Jesus Christ, whom you have sent" (John 17:3).

God created us to know Him in a deep and personal way.

I NEVER KNEW YOU

Besides the three levels of friendship, there are also strangers and enemies. In a biblical context, strangers were often regarded as enemies. "Depart from me, I never knew you" was a declaration of unaligned priorities. One of the most sobering passages in the Bible is found in Matthew 7:21-23. With these words, Jesus drew a line in religious activity's sand.

> "Not everyone who says to me, 'Lord, Lord,' will enter the kingdom of heaven, but only the one who does the will of my Father who is in heaven. Many will say to me on that day, 'Lord, Lord, did we not prophesy in your

name and in your name drive out demons and in your name perform many miracles?' Then I will tell them plainly, 'I never knew you. Away from me, you evildoers!'"

To more fully illustrate this danger, Jesus told a parable of a wedding feast attended by ten virgins. Five were ready for the bridegroom, but five discovered they were not. They were not prepared, even though they had been invited to the wedding feast. They further assumed they would be allowed in regardless, but they were sadly mistaken.

> "But while they were on their way to buy the oil, the bridegroom arrived. The virgins who were ready went in with him to the wedding banquet. And the door was shut. Later the others also came. 'Lord, Lord,' they said, 'open the door for us!' But he replied, 'Truly I tell you, I don't know you.'" (Matthew 25:10-12)

The greatest tragedy in this passage is that some people think they are ready to meet their God but are not. Perhaps they believe religious knowledge, church membership, and spiritual gifts will be enough, but they are sadly mistaken.

Can you imagine facing God on Judgment Day and hearing those words, "I never knew you"? Can you fathom the grief of being invited to the Marriage Supper of the Lamb and not being able to go in! Jesus warned that when He returned, many would be caught unprepared. He admonished us to be alert, watchful, and ready. I believe those who have a friendship with God will not be caught unaware.

If Jesus had engaged in social media, He would have had several acquaintances who called themselves friends but wouldn't qualify according to the biblical definition of friendship. Jesus was not willing to commit Himself to those who were unwilling to be more than acquaintances: "Now while he was in Jerusalem at the Passover Festival, many people saw the signs he was performing and believed in his name. But Jesus would not entrust himself to them, for he knew all people. He did not need any testimony about mankind, for he knew what was in each person" (John 2:23-25).

Jesus often tried to get His followers to deepen their level of relationship. Most Christians are familiar with the passage found in Revelation 3:20: "Behold, I stand at the door and knock. If anyone hears My voice and opens the door, I will come in to him and dine with him, and he with Me." Ironically, this is a message to Christians, not those who are lost. Jesus is pressing for a deeper relationship with those who bear His name.

We are all on this journey from neighbor to companion to friendship with God. Consider the three distinct sections of the Old Testament Tabernacle: the Outer Court, the Inner Court, and the Holy of Holies. The area that was closest to God was the Holy of Holies. Only the high priest would be allowed to visit God there. When Christ was crucified, the curtain separating the Holy of Holies from the world was torn. Symbolically, we all have access to this sacred place. The Outer Court is filled with neighbors. The Inner court with companions. The Holy of Holies is now for all His friends.

JACOB'S JOURNEY

Jacob's life is also a case study on moving from neighbor to companion to friend.

God appeared first to Jacob when he fled from his brother and went to his Uncle Laban's house. During the journey, God spoke to him through a dream and promised him many descendants. "When Jacob awoke from his sleep, he thought, 'Surely the LORD is in this place, and I was not aware of it'"

(Genesis 28:16). This encounter occurred in a place called Bethel, which means "house of God." Jacob began to develop a sense of spiritual destiny and personal connection with God in the house of God.

Jacob had another dream after several years. This time, God told him to leave the comforts and security of Laban's house and return to his homeland. This new direction would require Jacob to trust God more in his life and the lives of those under his care. (see Genesis 31:11-13). Through Jacob's obedience, he moved into a deeper companionship with God.

Jacob's third encounter with God occurred before his fearful meeting with his brother, Esau. Jacob believed his past had finally caught up with him, and there was no way out. In this moment of reckoning, God visited Jacob. Their encounter produced a severe struggle followed by a blessing. From that point on, Jacob suffered a limp but was given a new name, *Israel*, meaning "one who struggles with God" (see Genesis 32:24-28). No longer was he Jacob, which means "supplanter and deceiver."

This place of transformation was called *Peniel*, meaning "face of God." This was the connection God was seeking. Jacob had become a friend of God's. Jacob had successfully moved from neighbor to companion to intimate friendship.

THICK SKIN AND A SOFT HEART

Like Jacob, I believe we are all on a journey of friendship with God. Over the years, I have discovered that crises and suffering can move us from acquaintance to companion to friend. I experienced a loss of a ministry in 1989, a family tragedy in 2000, and a major health scare in 2011. All these were traumatic but ultimately brought me into a deeper intimacy with God. I may "limp" like Jacob, but I've also gained a stronger, more resilient relationship with Him. I like how Phillips Brooks characterizes the friendship we get to have with God through Jesus:

> "There is no power in the world like friendship. There is nothing, as you look upon your life, that has shaped you, made you what you are today, so completely as the friendships in which you have been living from your boyhood up. Now, Christianity seems to be simply the perfection of this power of friendship. It seems to be simply the opening of the sky so we can see that, above every other friendship, above everything that shapes our lives, there is the power of God made manifest in Jesus Christ, so that he who passes his life in utter and entire obedience to that of the Great Master enters into the character of that Master more and more."[13]

---

[13] Rev. J.B. McClure, *Pearls From Many Seas* (Rhodes & McClure Publishing Company, 1903), 205.

REFLECTION AND DISCUSSION

Please identify some of the people you would consider your neighbors or acquaintances.

_____

_____

_____

Regarding companions, who would qualify in your life? Why?

_____

_____

_____

Who are your closest friends? Why?

_____

_____

_____

How should we measure spiritual maturity?

_____

_____

_____

In this friendship journey, where is your current relationship with God?

_____

_____

_____

Chapter Three
Why a Good friend is Hard to Find

"Life isn't worth living, unless it is lived for someone else."
ALBERT EINSTEIN[14]

*Greater love has no one than this: to lay
down one's life for one's friends.*
JOHN 15:13

A FRIENDSHIP MEMORY

There was always a Dairy Queen in our small town, across the street from the high school.

Every kid looked forward to going to the Dairy Queen. Unlike most restaurants or drive-ins, all the items on the menu were appetizing. When our family went there, Dad typically ordered a chocolate malt. Mom would get a strawberry sundae. I would often get a malt like Dad but tried combining flavors such as pineapple/marshmallow or chocolate/strawberry. I remember even ordering a coffee malt one time.

---

[14] Goodreads, "Albert Einstein," last modified April 15,2025, https://www.goodreads.com/quotes/191974-life-isn-t-worth-living-unless-it-is-lived-for-someone.

One summer day, my friend Mitch and I rode our bikes to the Dairy Queen to get an ice cream. Standing at the counter, I noticed something new (or at least new to me): there were several sizes of malts. I had always purchased the smallest size, but that day I noticed several larger ones, and the biggest was a one-quart size that sold for fifty cents.

That seems like a ridiculously small amount today, but at the time, my weekly allowance was a quarter. So, this mountain of a malt was twice what I had in my pocket. I pointed out the malt to Mitch and asked him if he would be willing to pool his weekly allowance with mine (he got a quarter a week also), and together we could get the biggest malt in the world!

He agreed. So, the following week, after we both had received our allowances, we excitedly biked over to the Dairy Queen. We knew this was a once-in-a-lifetime epic event. We couldn't wait to tell the world what we had done together.

Everything went according to plan. We proudly ordered the malt (which I'm sure impressed even the Dairy Queen malt maker). We tried to wait patiently. But when the man finally brought the humongous chocolate malt to the counter, we just stood there and marveled. We had never seen a malt this big in our lives.

I had to be careful when I lifted it up because of its size. It was surprisingly heavy! Slowly, I made my way to the table behind us. We were both on the verge of screaming with delight when the bottom of the malt suddenly caught the edge of the table, flipping the entire malt contents all over the table.

Instantly, our joy turned to stunned silence as we saw our weekly allowance lost on a malt that had spilled before we even got a taste!

Friendships have those moments.

THE PRICE OF FRIENDSHIP

In 1983, I was reading *U.S. News and World Report* when I came across an article, "Why a Good Friend is Hard to Find." The article was an interview with Eugene Kennedy, a psychology professor at Loyola University. He had authored numerous books on human behavior, including *On Being a Friend*.

Because of God's invitation to me to be His friend, I was drawn to the article. As I read, I had an epiphany. *What would happen if we applied the same principles that exist in human friendships to our relationship with God?*

I learned a great deal from Kennedy's thinking. Notably, I discovered there are three pillars found in every good friendship: death, separation, and waiting.

DEATH

There are certain fundamentals that exist in human friendships that are often misunderstood. The first one is death. That may come as a surprise since friendship is generally a positive life-giving concept. But we need to consider this for a moment. Dr. Kennedy points out, "People want the rewards of friendship without the hazards of friendship, but you can't have one without the other. There's a death involved in every true act of friendship."[15] To be more specific,

> "Friendship is tested all the time by the small deaths, the almost unnoticed abrasions and wounds, so many of them unknowingly or unintentionally inflicted, that come so regularly in our contacts with each other . . .

---

[15] Eugene Kennedy, "Why a Good Friend is Hard to Find," *U.S. News and World Report*, September 26, 1983, 71.

Death to self begets friendship. Forgetting ourselves brings us that freedom—that open space in our entanglements—that makes love possible. That is the moment in which friendship surprises us. Friendship literally catches us off guard—when we are not preening ourselves to make an impression or protecting ourselves from the possibility of truly meeting someone else."[16]

I believe we can all relate to this in our hectic lives. Friends get sick and ask for our help. They get delayed in meeting us. Frequently, they can say or do something that offends. They require time and attention that we don't have. We seem to be constantly responding to subtle expectations, absorbing emotional elevations, and forced to give innumerable explanations. Sometimes, in our weaker moments, we ask ourselves if it is worth it. It is all so hard. We are tired and overwhelmed.

In the face of this, Professor Kennedy offers this insight: "Death is not a stranger to persons who understand that their fullest growth depends, not on grabbing everything for themselves, but on the readiness to give up much of themselves in loving self-sacrifice, in learning how to be friends. A willingness to die is always linked to the true discovery of life. Saint Paul spoke for everyone when he proclaimed, 'I die daily.'"[17]

LIVE TO GIVE

When it comes to the death of self, there is no greater example than the life of Christ. He died to Himself throughout His

---

[16] Eugene Kennedy, *On Being a Friend* (The Continuum Publishing Company, 1982), 36, 46.

[17] Ibid., 39.

ministry and then paid the ultimate price of death on the cross. Why?

To know us as His friend.

As Jesus made His way to Jerusalem for the final time, He became increasingly aware of the suffering He would soon face. Suddenly, His deep thoughts were interrupted by a painful cry, "Jesus, thou son of David, have mercy on me" (Luke 18:38, NKJV). Bartimaeus, the man who cried out, was blind but had heard that Jesus "the healer" was passing by. He was determined to catch Jesus' attention. The disciples quickly stepped in to control the situation. They told Bartimaeus to be quiet and leave Jesus alone. But he cried out again. To this earnest cry, Jesus stopped and called him to come. Jesus then took the time to see Bartimaeus' need and to hear his request. Then He healed him.

With the weight of the world on His shoulders, Jesus found time to help a stranger. Jesus always lived a life of mission and purpose. However, He was frequently interrupted in fulfilling it. It happened when a woman washed His feet with costly perfume, and in countless discussions with cynical religious teachers. It was in the oft-repeated attempts to explain the rudimentary principles of the Kingdom of God to His disciples. Jesus constantly put the needs of others above Himself. You can see this in His feeding of the 5,000 (Matthew 14:13-21), comforting the disciples at the Last Supper (Matthew 26:17-30), and, while He hung upon the cross, making sure His mother would be cared for (John 19:26-27). He lived His life for others, and He died for the sake of others.

AN INVITATION TO DIE

After Jesus declared He was the Messiah, He said to his disciples, "Whoever wants to be my disciple must deny themselves and take up their cross and follow me. For whoever wants to save their life will lose it, but whoever loses their life for me will find it" (Matthew 16:24-25). This declaration was not just a test of commitment for the disciples. Jesus didn't say this to gain control and dominion over His followers. I believe Jesus said this because He understood that we can't become friends unless we are willing to die. The disciples had to learn to die to themselves to enter this depth of friendship. Jesus was saying that you will not find life unless you are willing to live a life of self-sacrifice like me. This is an unavoidable qualification for a true friendship with God.

But He didn't stop there. Later He reminds His disciples, "Truly, truly I say to you, unless a grain of wheat falls into the earth and dies, **it remains alone**; but if it dies, it bears much fruit" (John 12:24). Jesus was explaining that if we are unwilling to die, we are destined to live a life of loneliness. We would do well to revisit these scriptures in our Bible studies and Sunday morning sermons. We have feasted on the sweet morsels of validation and affirmation without the hardy fare of death to self.

In Christ's admonition for us to die, He opened the door for His disciples to discover true friendship with Him. Let's not forget Dietrich Bonhoeffer's famous words, *"When Christ bids a man, he bids him come and die."*[18] Jesus well understands the connection between death and friendship. As a result, He was

---

[18] Goodreads, "Deitrich Bonhoeffer," last modified April 15, 2025, https://www.goodreads.com/quotes/98256-when-christ-calls-a-man-he-bids-him-come-and.

providing the disciples the keys to enjoy an eternal friendship with Him.

SEPARATION

The second fundamental aspect of friendship is separation. We are all familiar with the phrase, "Absence makes the heart grow fonder." This notion is well established in our culture. In fact, according to Kennedy, separation is the one thing we can be sure of in life.[19] I can certainly testify that being away from my fiancée, Martha, caused us to draw closer to one another during our engagement.

Our development into adulthood depends on our ability to remove ourselves from some individuals and connect with others. Dr. Kennedy explained, "There is a kind of death, a real separation for parents in seeing children grow up, a dying to themselves that is an extension of the love of their mothers and fathers who understand that separation is an urgent aspect of their lives."[20]

"Love that lasts needs the test of separation."[21] The Apostle Paul applied this foundational principle when he wrote to Philemon about his runaway slave, Onesimus. "Perhaps the reason he was separated from you for a little while was that you might have him back forever—no longer as a slave, but better than a slave, as a dear brother" (Philemon 15-16).

---

[19] Kennedy, *On Being a Friend,* 115.
[20] Ibid., 118.
[21] Ibid., 129.

FOR THE JOY

At the Last Supper, Jesus told His disciples that they were His friends but then explained that He would soon be separated from them (see John 16:16). From His perspective, this was not goodbye but the next step in an ever-deepening friendship. Although painful, Jesus saw the greater good in the separation. Eventually, His disciples saw the wisdom in it too. "There is another side to the ubiquitous mystery of separation. That is return, homecoming, the reunion of loved ones, the countless comings together whose meaning is heightened because of the separation that has been endured."[22]

On the day of His crucifixion, perhaps Jesus' most significant pain was in the separation that occurred with His Father. Jesus' final prayer was, "My God, my God, why have you abandoned me?" (Matthew 27:46, NLT). Jesus had experienced the bitter cup of separation, but there was hope mingled with sorrow, because he knew ". . . it was the LORD's good plan to crush him and cause him grief. Yet when his life is made an offering for sin, he will have many descendants. He will enjoy a long life, and the LORD's good plan will prosper in his hands" (Isaiah 53:10).

I don't know if you have noticed, but sometimes Jesus spoke in parable clusters. In other words, He shared more than one parable to illustrate a broader spiritual theme. You see this in Luke 15, where He shares three parables; the first is a lost sheep; the second, a lost coin; and the third, a lost son. When you look at them together, you discover spiritual insights that are not as evident in one parable alone.

---

[22] Ibid., 129.

For instance, collectively, there is a separation followed by a joyous reunion. In all three parables, there is a common thread of joy that the owner/father experiences whenever his lost treasure is finally found. This theme was significant because of the audience. Jesus was talking to tax collectors and sinners. He was trying to make a critical point; God considered them so valuable that He would be overjoyed if they were no longer separated from Him. What an incredibly important truth for them to see. It stood in stark contrast to that religious culture, which minimized their value.

LETTING GO

Few of us ever long for separation. Sure, we might cherish a few minutes alone before the kids come home from school, but even then, parents still feel the dread of anticipating the day their child will leave for college. But these are normal moments in our lives as we seek greater relationships and more valuable friendships. "In some way that passes understanding, separation seems essential if love is to achieve strength and fullness. Nothing pains us more than separation, and yet nothing confronts and challenges us more as we pursue the tasks of friendship that are the basic challenges of life."[23]

Sometimes we need to separate ourselves from ourselves. Sound impossible?

What I mean to say is that growth occurs when we let go of certain mindsets and understandings we've held onto. We need to separate ourselves from them to fulfill our destiny. In a spiritual sense, we stop growing when we get stuck in spiritual adolescence. "When I was a child, I talked like a child, I thought

---

[23] Ibid., 116.

like a child, I reasoned like a child. When I became a man, I put the ways of childhood behind me" (1 Corinthians 13:11). In a physical sense, you can't be a parent until you leave your childish ways. Likewise, in our spiritual development. "Brothers and sisters, I could not address you as people who live by the Spirit but as people who are still worldly—mere infants in Christ. I gave you milk, not solid food, for you were not yet ready for it. Indeed, you are still not ready. You are still worldly" (1 Corinthians 3:1-3).

WAITING

The third fundamental aspect of friendship is waiting. "Friends must understand waiting. There is no friendship without it."[24] "Part of loving others depends on being able to wait for them."[25] Sometimes, waiting seems more difficult than dying. We feel stuck and demand resolution. We get impatient and feel like we are in a holding pattern waiting to land. We battle the fear that we are not accomplishing anything. The Psalmist knew this angst well: "How long, O LORD? Will you forget me forever? How long will you hide your face from me? How long must I take counsel in my soul and have sorrow in my heart all the day? How long shall my enemy be exalted over me?" (Psalm 13:1-2). And what is our encouragement when we feel this way? "Wait for the LORD; be strong and take heart and wait for the LORD" (Psalm 27:14).

We must learn, like the Apostle Paul, to be content. But can we be content during a wait that has no predetermined ending? I suggest that we must. "There is more than a hint of death in waiting. We come up against restraint and the frustration of

---

24 Ibid., 137.
25 Ibid., 138.

our impulses in periods of waiting. We learn in our patience, according to the Bible, how to possess our souls."[26] Paul was waiting for his heavenly reward, and we should too. We should want and hope just as Paul did: "For through the Spirit we eagerly await by faith the righteousness for which we hope" (Galatians 5:5).

HATE TO WAIT

Consider the frustration when a close friend doesn't return your phone call or text. We surrender a portion of our spirits in each passing moment of waiting. In a fast-paced society, we find it more difficult to wait. Often, we don't like waiting in line. We don't like waiting in traffic. We don't like waiting in a restaurant.

We must learn to find contentment in the waiting, especially when it comes to God. This is where trust and patience are developed: "For the revelation awaits an appointed time; it speaks of the end and will not prove false. Though it linger, wait for it; it will certainly come and will not delay" (Habakkuk 2:3).

Abraham was a friend of God, but he had to learn to wait. There was a time when his impatience led him to Egypt, where he found nothing but trouble. Another time, he took matters into his own hands to get a son. This also led to trouble. Fortunately, he never gave up in his pursuit to be God's friend. As a result, the world has been blessed by his life and his descendants.

---

[26] Ibid., 137.

FAMOUS WAITERS

Jesus told his disciples to wait in Jerusalem until the promise of the Holy Spirit came. Once again, He was not trying to control their lives; He wanted to increase their friendship, and 120 of His disciples obeyed despite their lack of understanding. Only after Pentecost did it all make sense. And that deeper connection with God that came from death, separation, and waiting, prepared them for the promised arrival of the Holy Spirit, and helped reshape the world.

Hebrews 11 is often called the "Faith Chapter" because it defines faith and gives numerous examples of faith in action. Beginning with Abel, the author presents a chronological list of Old Testament heroes of the Christian faith. It is easy to be inspired by the faith they possessed.

But there is something else that is truly inspirational about their lives. Something that is generally missed or forgotten. Something that was linked to their faith. These Old Testament saints were willing to wait.

> "All these people were still living by faith when they died. They did not receive the things promised; they only saw them and welcomed them from a distance, admitting that they were foreigners and strangers on earth. People who say such things show that they are looking for a country of their own. If they had been thinking of the country they had left, they would have had opportunity to return. Instead, they were longing for a better country—a heavenly one. Therefore God is not ashamed to be called their God, for he has prepared a city for them." (Hebrews 11:13-16)

These men and women were willing to wait for God's promise for them. But this waiting was not confined to a few Old Testament saints. These were examples for us to live by. The Apostle Paul understood this spiritual principle. "For we know that if the earthly tent we live in is destroyed, we have a building from God, an eternal house in heaven, not built by human hands. Meanwhile we groan, **longing** to be clothed instead with our heavenly dwelling, because when we are clothed, we will not be found naked" (2 Corinthians 5:1-3).

Surprisingly, in describing the saints in heaven, there is also a need to wait. "When he opened the fifth seal, I saw under the altar the souls of those who had been slain because of the word of God and the testimony they had maintained. They called out in a loud voice, '**How long**, Sovereign Lord, holy and true, until you judge the inhabitants of the earth and avenge our blood?'" (Revelation 6:9-10).

THIS DO IN REMEMBRANCE OF ME

In many respects, the sacrament of Communion commemorates the death, separation, and waiting involved in our friendship with God. It reminds us of what Jesus went through to know us as His friend. It also reminds us of our patient separation but anticipated return of the one we love. Because of the significance of these truths, the Apostle Paul admonished the Church to consider their relational position with Christ: "So then, whoever eats the bread or drinks the cup of the Lord in an unworthy manner will be guilty of sinning against the body and blood of the Lord" (1 Corinthians 11:27). It would be a dishonor to Christ if anyone celebrated what He did for them but was unwilling to reciprocate the death, separation, and waiting He has endured.

ALTERNATIVE FRIENDSHIP

With the steep price of friendship, one may ask if friendship is worth it. Is it worth the cost? Professor Kennedy gives one final observation: "Friendship can be dangerous to your health. You cannot have a friendship that is all good times, joy, and laughter. When you enter a friendship, you have entered a field that limits you immediately. To sustain it, you have to be vulnerable and make sacrifices. A friend can hurt you—no question about that. If one chooses isolation from hurt, one also is choosing loneliness, and many people today have chosen that route."[27]

That's powerful, but I want to take this observation further. Today, millions are in a state of loneliness, even married couples. But people are quite adaptable. I believe some people have found a way to isolate themselves from hurt but mitigate the loneliness. These people have looked to animals and pets for emotional support. To be clear, not everyone who has a pet is suffering from loneliness or hurt. But I do believe some have used pets to help relieve loneliness and improve their mental health.

When it comes to a person's experience with the Church or Christians, many may have been hurt at one time or another. Sometimes, they stop attending and retreat from the Christian community. However, they continue to suffer an uneasy spiritual void. To compensate, several have tried to focus on other forms of spirituality. They have looked to New Age and other world religions. They have picked some *pet* religion or philosophy that doesn't require an elevated level of sacrifice. And every day, their heart is unsettled, because all of these false friends will never take the place of Jesus—their true friend.

---

[27] Eugene Kennedy, "Why a Good Friend is Hard to Find," *U.S. News and World Report*, September 26, 1983, 72.

FRIENDLY REPRISE

Do you see the implications of Dr. Kennedy's findings? If you do, you will see what is necessary to truly be someone's friend. In today's culture, many friendships lack depth and sustainability because of an unwillingness to pay the price.

The fundamentals of true friendship can greatly assist our relationship with God. What must we do to be God's friend? We must die to ourselves. Yes, we will suffer through times of separation from Him, and there will be times of waiting for Him to respond, but this is how we embrace the life that God is giving us and become friends of God.

How I have suffered because I didn't understand these fundamental truths. During dark and lonely days filled with self-doubt and frustration, I would often chastise myself, rebuke the devil, and work harder. Yet, these truths of friendship with God were hiding in plain sight. Jesus didn't hide His actions and words from us. In fact, I believe many of Jesus' seemingly difficult teachings were designed to deepen our relationship with Him. Unfortunately, many of His followers—me included—initially missed this.

It is critical that we understand God's work in our lives so that we don't suffer emotional and spiritual setbacks in our walk with Him. We must learn to embrace our spiritual blessing of being a friend of God despite our hatred of death, separation, and waiting. We can learn to walk hand in hand with Jesus through it all.

REFLECTION AND DISCUSSION

Please identify a childhood memory with a friend. What part of this story makes you happy or sad?

_____

_____

_____

How can we die to ourselves for the sake of a friendship with God?

_____

_____

_____

Was there a time when you experienced a separation from God? Please explain what happened.

_____

_____

_____

Share a time when you had to wait for God.

_____

_____

_____

Chapter Four
Drink of the Cup

"Drinking the cup is an act of selfless love, an act of immense trust, an act of surrender to a God who will give what we need when we need it."
HENRI NOUWEN[28]

Going a little farther, he fell with his face to the ground and prayed, 'My Father, if it is possible, may this cup be taken from me. Yet not as I will, but as you will.'
MATTHEW 26:39

With a deeper understanding of the cost of friendship, let us look at Christ's final hours from this perspective.

In the book of John, we have the most detailed account of Christ's final hours with His disciples. While we don't know the exact time between the Last Supper and His arrest in the Garden of Gethsemane, some scholars believe it was around seven hours. It was a time in this world like no other. About three hours were spent in dining and meaningful fellowship

---

[28] Goodreads, "Can you drink the cup?," last modified April 4, 2025, https://www.goodreads.com/work/quotes/666209-can-you-drink-the-cup#:~:text=Henri%20J.M.%20Nouwen%2C%20Can%20You%20Drink%20the%20Cup%3F,-likes%3A%200&text=Drinking%20the%20cup%20is%20an,need%20when%20we%20need%20it.

with those closest to Jesus. Throughout the time, eternity was on His lips. Everything He shared had a heightened sense of purpose and passion. After their last meal, about an hour was spent travelling from the house where they met to the garden located at the base of the Mount of Olives. The remaining three hours were spent there in prayer. Let's look at these seven critical hours more carefully, starting with the Passover meal.

EVENTIDE

Jesus eagerly wanted to celebrate the Passover with His disciples. "When the hour came, Jesus and his apostles reclined at the table. And he said to them, 'I have eagerly desired to eat this Passover with you before I suffer'" (Luke 22:14-15). All the prior Passovers in Israel were now culminating in this Passover meal. Jesus' disciples knew that through the death of a sacrificial lamb, God's people were to be separated from a pagan land, go through a wilderness season, and find an ultimate rest in the Promise Land. What they struggled to understand was that Jesus was their sacrificial Lamb of God.

In John 14, Jesus focused on comforting His disciples: He was more concerned about their feelings than His impending suffering. His love for them transcended His fear of death. He listened to their hearts and wanted to reassure them regarding the coming dramatic changes.

Then, in John 15, Jesus bestowed upon His disciples an incredible honor, saying, "I no longer call you servants, because a servant does not know his master's business. Instead, I have called you friends, for everything that I learned from my Father I have made known to you" (John 15:15).

Let's consider for a moment what Jesus gave them. It certainly was different than what other leaders typically give. Jesus would have given them bonuses if He had been their corporate boss. If He had been their college professor, He would have given them diplomas. And if Jesus were the military commander many of His disciples wanted Him to be, He would have given them all medals.

But Jesus gave them something you can't hold in your hand, only in your heart. He gave them a new relationship. He called them His friends. Jesus gave the greatest gift He could have given. It wasn't eternal life. It wasn't His earthly life; it was His heart. The disciples came to Jesus initially as followers of a Rabbi. They became His servants. But now, Jesus no longer felt that *servant* accurately described their relationship—He now considered them *friends.*

It is important to realize that friendship didn't begin with Jesus' humanity. His longing for closeness with His friends wasn't a new desire that He had to deal with once He came to earth. Friendship originated from the heart of God: it has always been there. Our desire for friendship came from Him, not the other way around. Friendship was His ultimate gift to us!

DARK NIGHT OF THE SOUL

Around 10:00 p.m., Jesus and His disciples left the house to go to the Garden of Gethsemane just northeast of Jerusalem. Jesus knew they were entering a time of danger and transition. Unfortunately, the disciples failed to grasp the importance of the moment. Peter had pledged his loyalty and fidelity, forsaking any notion of betrayal or abandonment. And while John did not note it in his Gospel, I'm sure many of the disciples felt the same way. But that incongruency didn't weaken Jesus' desire to be with them as long as possible. It is noteworthy that outside of the Godhead, Jesus had never had this level of friendship with anyone in the universe. It was a unique and deeply personal connection for Jesus. Surely more for Him than for them.

From 11:00 p.m. to 2:00 a.m., while in the garden, Jesus brought three of His closest disciples to an isolated place for a time of prayer—for their benefit as much as for His. However, they again failed to grasp the gravity of the situation and soon fell asleep. Jesus made a point of waking Peter and exhorted him, "What! Could you not watch with Me one hour?" (Matthew 26:40, NKJV).

Assuming a person can be hurt to the degree that they love, who hurt Jesus the most on the night He was arrested? Was it Judas? The religious rulers? Pontius Pilate? No, I believe it was Peter. It was his failure to understand what Christ was warning him about. Yet, Jesus remained focused on the well-being of His friend.

It was at this time that Jesus cried out, "Father, if you are willing, take this cup from me; yet not my will, but yours be done" (Luke 22:42). Most Christians interpret "this cup" to be Christ's anticipated physical suffering. I have no problem with that interpretation. However, let me suggest an additional consideration. Could it be possible that Jesus' request of His Father was not for an alternative to physical suffering but an alternative to the emotional pain due to the separation from His friends?

Several years ago, my daughter Molly authored a poem about Christ in the Garden of Gethsemane. We decided to record it at the home studio of a friend. As we did, the Lord's presence brought it to life. We had an encounter with Jesus that still melts my heart. When we finished the recording, we had her basic poem and a description of what God was showing us. Hopefully, you will catch the Lord's heart cry in it.

DRINK OF THE CUP

Will thou drink of this cup of suffering?
Will thou drink of this cup of shame?
Wilt thou give up a life of pleasure,
For a life of sorrow and pain?

You can almost see Him—there in the garden. The clouds, for the most part, cover the moon and stars. But every once in a while, there is a break. You can see His image in the distance. His face is filled with emotion. He knows what is about to occur. He is anxious for others to see what He sees, but so many are asleep; they're not aware; they can't see in the dark.

Can thou dieth a death of anguish,
Amidst souls undone?
Can thou sweat drops of blood in travail?
Then draw nigh, my Beloved, come.
Sharest my deepest groanings?
Beatest your heart with mine?
Walk in a grace unshakable.
Walk in a love divine.

I see His hand extended. His eyes catch mine. What do I do? His invitation to me is to dance with Him. To embrace Him; to have my heartbeat with His; to feel what He feels; to see what He sees. I must respond. His eyes demand an answer.

Draw nigh, my Beloved, come. Dance with a love divine.

Do you see them? Do you see the undone souls all around you? Do you see them? Can you travail with Me? Then come nigh, my Beloved, come. My Beloved, come.
Will you drink of the cup? Then draw nigh, my Beloved, come. Come, my Beloved, and dance with Me.

CONDITIONAL SURRENDER

Around 2:00 a.m., Roman soldiers, led by Judas, came to arrest Jesus. Jesus' heart for His friends was clearly evident. He would submit Himself to the guards under one condition: that they let His friends go free. "Jesus answered, 'I told you that I am he. If you are looking for me, then let these men go'" (John 18:8).

After releasing the disciples, they bound Jesus and took Him to the house of Annas and then to Caiaphas, the high priest. John the disciple, who was known to the high priest, was able to enter the courtyard and obtained permission for Peter to be admitted (see John 18:15-16). This is where Peter's denial occurred. "Just as he was speaking, the rooster crowed. **The Lord turned and looked straight at Peter**. Then Peter remembered the word the Lord had spoken to him: 'Before the rooster crows today, you will disown me three times.' And he went outside and wept bitterly" (Luke 22:60-62). Jesus' look brought Peter to tears.

Early in the morning, Jesus was sent to Pontius Pilate. The Roman governor was amazed at Jesus' lack of answers to His questions. Pilate must have thought, "Surely, Jesus is naïve to what is going on. Poor man, He just doesn't get what is at stake for Him." Jesus quite possibly was thinking the same thing about him!

Pilate's wife entered the scene unexpectedly and told him of a troubling dream she had about Jesus. She implored her husband to release him.

So many times, angry mobs and crowds of religious leaders sought to rid themselves of the "prophet from Nazareth." Numerous times, those who were offended by Jesus sought to kill Him. Each time, during the ministry of Christ, He escaped unharmed. Not this time. In this case, Jesus chose not to take advantage of the opportunity; He intentionally laid His life down for His friends—that was His desired destiny.

STRANGERS BECOME FRIENDS AT THE CROSS

Recently, I watched the movie *The Passion* with my grandson. It had been ten years since I last saw it. Near the end of the movie, I again witnessed the depiction of Christ's painful crucifixion. As I felt the gravity of the moment, I listened to His brief dialogue with the two thieves and was struck with an amazing thought: strangers become friends at the cross.

It is in brokenness and humility that the best friendships are forged. If we want to be a friend of God, a good place to start is at the cross. Not to just witness it, but to be on it. Not to just watch it, but to feel it. At the cross, we are compelled to die to our selfishness and pride. To humble ourselves before a perfect king who suffered such painful injustice on our behalf.

The one thief, who experienced a change of heart, received an incredible reward as revealed in these words: "Then he said, 'Jesus, remember me when you come into your kingdom.' Jesus answered him, 'Truly I tell you, today you will be with me in paradise'" (Luke 23:42-43). I have read this passage many times in my life as a follower of Jesus, and each time I have always emphasized the amazing gift of grace through the lens of time. I always took note of Jesus' promise of today: "Today you will be in paradise." But this time, watching the story unfold, I noticed something different, and dare I say, better. To the thief on the cross, Jesus promised, "Today you will be **with me** in paradise." Jesus gave a convicted thief something more than eternal life. He gave him the gift of eternal friendship!

As for how wonderful this moment was for both of them, an old hymn has touched my heart for years and reminds me of Christ's love for all of us.

WHEN I SURVEY THE WONDEROUS CROSS

Isaac Watts

When I survey the wondrous cross
On which the Prince of glory died,
My richest gain I count but loss,
And pour contempt on all my pride.

Forbid it, Lord, that I should boast,
Save in the death of Christ my God!
All the vain things that charm me most,
I sacrifice them to His blood.

See from His head, His hands, His feet,
Sorrow and love flow mingled down!
Did e'er such love and sorrow meet,
Or thorns compose so rich a crown?

Were the whole realm of nature mine,
That were a present far too small;
Love so amazing, so divine,
Demands my soul, my life, my all.

JOY OF SACRIFICE

For good to prosper, sacrifices must be made. For evil to prosper, only indifference is required. This might be axiomatic, and there are many versions of this in the ethos, particularly as it relates to politics and civil discourse, but as I look at my life, and the lives of countless others, I contend it is true.

Think about all the good you have experienced in life. Do you see all the sacrifices that undergird your happiness? Your desires? Your many blessings? Our parents, teachers, doctors, law enforcement, and countless others have contributed to your happiness. Think of the challenging work needed to bring your food from the garden to the grocery store. Consider all the burdens related to the manufacturer of your clothes. These individuals didn't necessarily give their lives for you but played a part in your prosperity.

This world would not exist for very long if we didn't have people willing to make sacrifices. We may dream of a self-indulgent lifestyle, but it isn't practical. Sacrifice is required for humankind to exist and progress.

If this is an unavoidable truth, then a key to life is discovering a joy in sacrifice. Joy in sacrifice is finding contentment in giving up something you love for something you love even more. This was the case with Jesus, and He invites us to do the same. "For the joy set before him he endured the cross, scorning its shame, and sat down at the right hand of the throne of God" (Hebrews 12:2). There are many in this world who have not accepted Him as their personal Savior who still appreciate what He did. Certainly, no one has ever lived a life like He did. Yet most would argue that the world would be much better if we lived like Him.

What does it look like to live like Jesus? How can we assess what sacrifice is and when it happens? I don't think it is always as grand as dying on a cross; rather, it could happen when a bowl filled with apples is passed around the table, and instead of choosing the finest one, you select one of lesser quality, preferring that someone else will be able to enjoy it. It's getting up in the middle of the night to feed the baby. It is going to school even when we don't feel like it. It could be as simple as finding more joy in others opening their presents on Christmas Day than your own. "Pleasure, relatively easy to come by, never measures up to joy, which seldom comes without pain but which has a timeless quality to it."[29]

In the previous chapter, we looked at the cost of friendship. Many would admit their own failure to pay that cost consistently—sacrificing for the well-being of others. May I suggest that the strength and motivation to become true friends come from the joy of sacrifice? This is what gave Jesus the strength He needed to finish His task on earth. He lived with joy. He sacrificed with joy. He gave with joy. Like Jesus, we must learn to live to give!

JESUS WEPT

Only a few families in the Bible had numerous interactions with Jesus: Peter's family was one. James and John's family was another. And then there was a woman named Mary who anointed Jesus' feet. She had a sister and a brother. The three of them would get to know Jesus as their friend.

One day, the brother, Lazarus, got deathly sick. Word went out to Jesus to please come and heal him. Jesus was strangely delayed but eventually came. However, by the time He arrived, it was too late—Lazarus was dead. Surprisingly, this did not discourage Jesus. To Him, Lazarus was still restorable. What is noteworthy is Jesus' reaction.

> "When Mary reached the place where Jesus was and saw him, she fell at his feet and said, 'Lord, if you had been here, my brother would not have died.' When Jesus saw her weeping, and the Jews who had come along with her

---

[29] Kennedy, *On Being a Friend*, 126.

also weeping, he was deeply moved in spirit and troubled. 'Where have you laid him?' he asked. 'Come and see, Lord,' they replied. Jesus wept. Then the Jews said, 'See how he loved him!'" (John 11:32-36)

You could sum up Jesus' love for His friends in the shortest verse in the Bible—*Jesus wept*. I believe Jesus still weeps with His friends.

JESUS STILL WEEPS

There was a time when I had the task of closing a ministry. It was particularly painful because it was my whole life for seventeen years. I met my wife there. Our two children were born while in the ministry. As I wrestled in prayer about it all, I got a vision of Jesus. To my surprise, He was weeping.

I was taken aback at the impact my suffering had on Jesus. I expected Him to pat me on the back and tell me the whole ordeal was really not so bad. But that wasn't the case. He was weeping with me. This spiritual moment with Jesus gave me a deeper appreciation of His heart and care more than any words of wisdom and comfort I received from others at the time. I saw vividly that His heart was broken over the things that broke my heart. He had entered my sufferings.

Several years later, I was facing another painful situation. Someone I loved deeply had drifted from the Lord. My heart was broken for them and God. Suddenly, I had another vision of me embracing Jesus and sobbing on His shoulder. To my surprise, He was doing the same on my shoulder. We were crying on each other's shoulders. Once again, I was amazed at the level of Jesus' involvement in my suffering.

When we are hurting, nothing is better than having a friend by our side. It may have been after a car crash. It could have been an unexpected death in the family. It could have been a cancer diagnosis. Whatever the crisis, a friend is a welcome source of strength and comfort: ". . . lo, I am with you always, even to the end of the age" (Matthew 28:20, NKJV).

IN THE GARDEN

C. Austin Miles

I come to the garden alone,
While the dew is still on the roses,
And the voice I hear falling on my ear
The Son of God discloses.

Refrain:
And He walks with me, and He talks with me,
And He tells me I am His own;
And the joy we share as we tarry there,
None other has ever known.

He speaks, and the sound of His voice
Is so sweet the birds hush their singing,
And the melody that He gave to me
Within my heart is ringing. *[Refrain]*

I'd stay in the garden with Him,
Though the night around me be falling,
But He bids me go; through the voice of woe
His voice to me is calling. *[Refrain]*[30]

---

[30] Hymnary.org, "I Come to the Garden Alone," last modified April 16, 2025, https://hymnary.org/text/i_come_to_the_garden_alone.

REFLECTION AND DISCUSSION

What does it mean to drink of the cup of Christ's suffering?

_____

_____

_____

Explain the joy of sacrifice.

_____

_____

_____

Have you ever noticed God's response to your suffering? Describe the experience.

_____

_____

_____

As we have explored Jesus' love for His friends, what can we learn about His love for us?

_____

_____

_____

Chapter Five
No Greater Love

"May the Lamb that was slain receive the reward of His suffering."
MORAVIAN MISSIONARY CALL [31]

For I resolved to know nothing while I was with you except Jesus Christ and him crucified.
1 CORINTHIANS 2:2

In Paul's letter to the church in Corinth, he expressed his ambition to know Christ and His crucifixion. Why was Christ's crucifixion so important to him? Why did he declare, "May I never boast except in the cross of our Lord Jesus Christ, through which the world has been crucified to me, and I to the world" (Galatians 6:14)? Paul saw the cross at the heart of the gospel and the cornerstone of a friendship with God.

The Scriptures reveal that the greatest act of love is for someone to die for their friends. Thankfully, this is still the belief in our post-Christian culture. We continue to honor those who do so. The heart of the Gospel is the death of Jesus on the cross. Those who attend church often hear and accept this

---

[31] TBC staff, "May the Lamb that was Slain Receive the Reward of His Suffering," *The Berean Call*, June 3, 2014, https://www.thebereancall.org/content/may-lamb-was-slain-receive-reward-his-sufferings?.

historical fact, but few understand the dynamics and implications of Jesus' death. To know Jesus as a friend, we need a better understanding of what He did for us on the cross. Many scholars refer to this sacred subject as the Atonement, a word many of us are familiar with but have a challenging time defining. According to Albert Barnes, who wrote a classic on the subject, "An atonement is, properly, *an arrangement by which the literal infliction of the penalty due to sin may be avoided*; it is something which may be *substituted* in the place of punishment; it is that which will answer the same end which would be secured by the literal infliction of the law."[32]

POWER IN THE BLOOD

I find it interesting that the concept of an atonement appears in the earliest records of humankind. Abel presented a sacrifice to the Lord that included the fat portions from the firstborn of his flock (see Genesis 4:4). The sacrifice of an animal of value pleased the Lord. On the other hand, Cain's presented a sacrifice of fruit to the Lord (see Genesis 4:3). This was not pleasing to God. Why? It did not involve the shedding of blood. Throughout history, cultures have used the shedding of blood to appease their gods. Who taught them this? How did it become such a universally accepted practice? How did it ever enter the mind of humans that sacrificing a life of value may secure forgiveness for wrongdoing from their deity? The need for a blood sacrifice appears to be hardwired into the conscience of humans.

---

[32] Albert Barnes, *The Atonement* (Bethany Fellowship Inc., 1860), 230.

LEGAL ADVICE

An unusual place to discover the dynamics of the Atonement is in the courtroom, through the lens of the fundamental laws of justice. These laws were put in place to protect us—the general public. Overall, that's a good thing, but it does have some fundamental limitations according to Winkie Pratney:

- Laws cannot pardon. They can only sentence.
- Laws cannot justify. They have no power to make the criminal right. Laws can only state that the lawbreaker is wrong.
- Laws cannot sanctify. They have no power to make the criminal good. They cannot change their lives.[33]

Attached to the laws are obvious penalties. This keeps laws from becoming only advice. A penalty shows the value or importance of the law. For example, there is a higher penalty for murder than for a parking ticket. Early Jewish law reflected this: "If anyone injures his neighbor, as he has done it shall be done to him, fracture for fracture, eye for eye, tooth for tooth; whatever injury he has given a person shall be given to him" (Leviticus 24:19-20).

When a person is found guilty of breaking the law, there is an expectation that the penalty will be imposed on them. We call this justice. However, something can be given upon sentencing of the lawbreaker that sets aside justice. It is referred to as mercy or pardon. I believe mercy is found in the heart of God. "But because of his great love for us, God, who is rich in mercy, made us alive with Christ even when we were dead in transgressions—it is by grace you have been saved" (Ephesians 2:4-5).

---

[33] Winkie Pratney, The Atonement, Agape Force, sound cassette.

Mercy is a wonderful concept. For some reason, in the heart of most people, there is a desire for mercy to be extended whenever possible. People often feel good when someone facing a harsh penalty suddenly has their penalty reduced. Albert Barnes states, "There has been everywhere a deep conviction that pardon *should* in certain cases be extended to the guilty; but *how* it can be done so as to secure the interests of justice, so as to maintain the power of the law, and so as not to be an encouragement for the commission of crime, is a point which has never been settled in any human administration."[34]

An example of this would be the story of Jonathan inadvertently breaking King Saul's foolish decree. Saul said, "'May God deal with me, be it ever so severely, if you do not die, Jonathan.' But the men said to Saul, 'Should Jonathan die—he who has brought about this great deliverance in Israel? Never! As surely as the LORD lives, not a hair of his head will fall to the ground, for he did this today with God's help.' So the men rescued Jonathan, and he was not put to death" (1 Samuel 14:44-45). Those who fought with Jonathan rose up and defended him. As a result, his life was spared. His father, King Saul, reversed his decree and granted him a pardon.

Mercy is beautiful, but it does have a weakness. Whenever mercy is granted, justice suffers. When mercy is given freely, society becomes weaker, and the public becomes less safe. "It gives offenders a double hope of escaping punishment; a hope they will not be caught and if caught and convicted, to receive pardon."[35]

There is another problem that a human justice system faces. Neither justice nor mercy rehabilitate the guilty person. Neither

---

[34] Ibid., 48.
[35] Winkie Pratney, The Atonement, Agape Force, sound cassette.

guarantees future good behavior. The concept of atonement is giving mercy to a guilty party by having someone else suffer on their behalf. In history, this has been attempted occasionally. Often, it was a wealthy person paying someone else to take their place. Once again, the problem is that the guilty person is not changed for the better. If anything, they become more comfortable breaking the law.

THE JUDGE'S CHALLENGE

God's moral laws are not inventions but descriptions of reality. Wisdom is to conform; sin is to rebel (see Proverbs 8). Now, it was always in the heart of the Father to extend mercy to those who broke His laws. However, justice would suffer if our Heavenly Father extended mercy to everyone. No one would respect the law, and our world would fall apart. Attached to God's laws are penalties. Without the penalties, the laws would only be advice.

All this background is essential when considering the implications of Jesus' death. The Bible states that sin is the transgression of the law. "Everyone who sins is breaking God's law, for all sin is contrary to the law of God" (1 John 3:4, NLT). So, what could God do to best ensure the future good conduct of those guilty of breaking His moral laws? Personally demonstrate His love for both the law and the lawbreaker. And to do this, God had to be personally involved in a substitutionary act of atonement. According to Pratney, the substitute must

1. be an uncompromising friend of the government;
2. be an uncompromising friend of the dishonored law. He must protect it by showing its value and how evil it is to violate it;
3. be the compassionate friend of the sinner;

4. be righteous, that is, he must be clear of any complicity in the crime of the sinner. There must be no charge or suspicion of guilt resting on him;

5. be willing to volunteer for a gratuitous service. He must not be a hostage;

6. be held once in eternity and once in the universe because it must be the most important thing that ever happened. It must be the only thing of its kind. Because it is so significant, it cannot ever happen again.[36]

ACCEPTABLE PAYMENT OR ACCEPTABLE SUBSTITUTE?

Most people accept the fact that Jesus died for our sins. Most believe it was a substitutionary death in the sense that He took the punishment we deserved. However, in doing so, Christ was either satisfying the debt to the Father or making a way for the Father to extend mercy without sacrificing His justice. Christ's death was either a literal acceptance of our punishment or an acceptable substitute for our punishment. It can't be both. Let's explore what the Bible reveals.

God laid the groundwork for Christ's atonement in the Old Testament. God cursed the land because of Saul's sin against the Gibeonites (see 2 Samuel 21:1-2). To reconcile the situation, seven descendants of Saul were sacrificed. This was not a literal eye-for-an-eye transaction, but it was sufficient to remedy the hurt and pain of the Gibeonites, and the Lord healed the land. Afterward, God listened to the people's prayers (see 2 Samuel 21:14).

---

[36] Winkie Pratney, The Atonement, Agape Force, sound cassette.

When David sinned against the Lord by having Israel's fighting men counted, he became conscience-stricken and confessed his sin before the Lord. David was then given the unusual opportunity of choosing one of three possible punishments (see 1 Samuel 24:12). After choosing one, the punishment began. However, God chose to extend mercy before it was completed (see 1 Samuel 24:16).

The punishment was not a literal payment. If so, God would not have been able to mitigate it. Consequences were reduced because of God's mercy. However, David's humility and confession played into God's decision.

Consider the parable of a servant being forgiven a great debt by the king (see Matthew 18:21-35). The story didn't say a man came along and paid the servant's debt. No, it told us the king erased the debt because he was merciful.

Despite these illustrations from Scripture, many Christians today speak of Christ paying the debt for our sins, paying the price for our sins, or satisfying the wrath of God. However, I see several problems with this position:

- It paints a picture of the Father being wrathful and the Son being merciful. The Godhead is not in unity but in disagreement.
- It does not reflect the Old Testament sacrificial system. God did not pour out His wrath on the animals in place of the Israelites. He didn't vent His righteous judgment on the animals, sending them to hell in place of the Israelites. On the contrary, they were killed honorably and as painlessly as possible.
- Sin is treated as a debt to be paid rather than a crime to be pardoned. For example, consider a man who is found guilty of a crime, and the penalty is a fine of $10,000. If someone stepped forward and paid the penalty for his

crime, the guilty man would be set free without any further repercussions. He would no longer need mercy. In fact, he could demand justice.

By implication, this position does not demand a change of heart on the part of the sinner. The sinner does not need to show remorse and repent of his sin. He would only have to accept that someone paid for his sin. If Christ paid for our sins, forgiveness is no longer necessary. "When a debt is paid, there is not forgiveness; when a penalty is endured, there is no mercy."[37] Christ becomes a benefactor more than a friend.

In addition, I have heard devotees of this position declare that Jesus has forgiven our sins, past, present, *and* future. This would be like a man confessing his crime of robbing a local bank before the judge. To the shock of everyone in the courtroom, the judge declares, "I pardon you for this crime and any future robberies you commit!" What message does the judge's declaration send to the bank robber? What message does it send to the bank that was robbed? To the local citizens who do their business at that bank?

HIS PAIN, OUR GAIN

Regarding the substitutionary atonement, Barnes states, "It is not a commercial transaction—a matter of debt and payment, of profit and loss. It pertains to law, to government, to holiness; not to literal debt and payment. Sin is crime, not debt; it is guilt, not a failure in a pecuniary obligation."[38] By allowing Jesus to die on the cross, God could extend mercy without weakening the law, provided certain *conditions* were met. These

---

[37] Barnes, *The Atonement*, 231.
[38] Ibid., 230.

conditions would not be the grounds for His mercy. The grounds or foundation of mercy would remain in the heart of God. These would merely be His reasonable *conditions* to be met by those seeking divine pardon. Allow me to explain.

Consider a typical family situation. Little Billie has been warned not to take any cookies from the cookie jar. However, the next day, his mother notices that the cookie jar has far fewer cookies. She confronts little Billie, who denies any involvement. The longer Billie maintains his innocence, while hiding the cookies conspicuously behind his back, the more his mother will be moved towards justice. She alone has the power to extend mercy to her son, but she knows that it would not be wise to do so unless there was a change in Billie's heart.

A judge can be presented with numerous reasons for extending mercy to a guilty person, but those reasons do not force him to do so. Before making a final decision, the judge carefully considers the current attitude of the guilty person towards their crime. The decision ultimately is made from the inner considerations of the judge's mind and heart.

Likewise, the mercy of God is the grounds of our salvation and can never be earned. However, God is inclined to extend mercy if reasonable conditions are met. That is divine wisdom. Listed below are the frequently mentioned biblical conditions:

RECOVERY OF LOST PERFECTION

1. *Admission of guilt (confession)*. The longer a person denies their crime, the more a judge will move towards justice. Prior to my conversion, I was encouraged to write a list of the things I had done wrong. Doing so helped me realize how much I had disobeyed and hurt God. I knew I couldn't hide or justify my sins any longer. "Whoever

conceals their sins does not prosper, but the one who confesses and renounces them finds mercy" (Proverbs 28:13).

2. *Awareness of the gravity of your crime (sincere sorrow). Shortly after I confessed my sins, I became aware of the gravity of my selfishness. I experienced deep regret and brokenness.* "Godly sorrow brings repentance that leads to salvation and leaves no regret, but worldly sorrow brings death. See what this godly sorrow has produced in you: what earnestness, what eagerness to clear yourselves, what indignation, what alarm, what longing, what concern, what readiness to see justice done" (*2 Corinthians 7:10-11*).

3. *Turn from your crime (repentance).* I learned that God will not deliver me from sins I still hold onto. He doesn't repent for us. Tears are not repentance. Judas wept bitterly but didn't repent. I also realized that I must be willing to make full restitution if possible. "Repent, then, and turn to God, so that your sins may be wiped out, that times of refreshing may come from the Lord" (Acts 3:19).

4. *A person must promise that they will be a loyal citizen (faith) in the future.* I saw the need to make a complete change in the direction of my life. Now, I needed to be loyal to God and His Word. "If you declare with your mouth, 'Jesus is Lord,' and believe in your heart that God raised him from the dead, you will be saved" (Romans 10:9).

The Atonement was not just an ingenious way for God to forgive humans who had sinned. It was also an effective means of breaking down our rebellion and motivating us to start trusting Him with our lives. For God, there always remains a risk in this. Some may still rebel and resist. But God would never make obedience compulsory by robbing us of our free moral choice. What is forced can never love. Instead, He sought to win our hearts and secure our friendship by demonstrating His sacrificial love for us. From the beginning, He has only had our highest good as His heart's desire. There is no vindictiveness or unappeased wrath found in God.

SO, WHY THE FUSS?

Why is holding a biblical view of the Atonement so significant? Today, I see countless numbers of professing Christians struggling with sin. Many have turned to theological teachings that give them comfort and security to find relief. They fail to see the importance of changing their hearts to receive mercy from the Judge of the Universe. Throughout the Scriptures, those who were broken and humble received God's grace. "God opposes the proud but shows favor to the humble" (James 4:6).

A lack of remorse and repentance forms a weak connection with God. As a result, many have gotten stuck in the "acquaintance" stage. While they struggle to hold onto their faith, they begin to doubt whether it is working for them. Someone is to blame, and God is often falsely identified as the failing party. However, the underlying problem is that many professing Christians have never met the reasonable conditions for His mercy: "The sacrifice you desire is a broken spirit. You will not reject a broken and repentant heart, O God" (Psalm 51:17, NLT). This was the key to King David's restoration of friendship with God. He was restored because he met God's conditions for mercy.

TAKING GOD'S SIDE

For several years, there has been a focus in our culture on accepting and forgiving ourselves. Unfortunately, this has led many to make peace with sin in their lives. The Apostle John clearly states, "No one who lives in him keeps on sinning. No one who continues to sin has either seen him or known him" (1 John 3:6), and "We know that anyone born of God does not continue to sin; the One who was born of God keeps them safe, and the evil one cannot harm them" (1 John 5:18). The Apostle John reminds us that when we meet God's conditions for forgiveness, we no longer accept sin as part of our identity. Sin becomes an exception rather than the rule of our lives. Our hearts have now become aligned with God's. As His friend, we will continue to hate what He hates and love what He loves (see Romans 12:9).

THE FATHER JUDGE

Shortly after my conversion, I heard Winkie Pratney speak on the Atonement. At the end of his teaching, he shared a story that impacted me greatly. I trust it will bless you as well.

Say that you were a father, and you really loved your son. And you were also a judge, and your son committed a crime of the century. He murdered fifty people, one by one, and buried them in an apple orchard.

And you find this out, and you're his father, and you're also the judge (now they arrange it in American courts so that no father can try his own children or relative). Imagine if you were the ultimate judge of the universe, and you had to.

Now, what do you do? On one hand, you really do love your son; you really do care about him. On the other hand, can you just simply stand up in front of the court and say, "Well, I understand, but he's my son."

They deliberate the facts; they find that there were no extenuating circumstances. This kid committed cold-blooded murder, with no possible way of showing pardon. The jury comes back, and they say, "He is guilty, and we recommend the death sentence."

What do you say? Now you're the judge, you're the one who has the power to reverse that verdict. What do you do? Your son is standing there before you; he's looking up at you. You're the dad, and you look at him and you love him. And you look at the whole court, who are saying, "This kid is going to have to pay for that." "My wife was killed by this kid." "My little daughter was killed by this kid." "My husband was shot." "My son was killed by this man."

Do you see that? What are you going to do? Well, I'll tell you what the Judge of the Universe did. He came forward, and the kid, knowing a little bit about what the judge was like, knowing and sensing deep down inside that maybe his father cared about him, expects to be pardoned. He stands there, looking up at his dad, thinking, "My dad will spring me." How many sinners do you know who think that? At the last moment, God will come in and He won't hurt me.

The judge comes up and you know what he says, "I find my son guilty as charged, and I sentence him to execution right here in the courtroom in the next five minutes."

Now, what does that do to the son? Shock! "Wow, you mean my dad put aside all his feelings and stuck to the law? I thought he would get me out." He doesn't believe it; he thought maybe the court would get hung up and go on for years until finally he would just get a light sentence.

But the dad says, "Right now." And they bring in the gas chamber right there in the middle of the court.

Now, what does the kid do? Suddenly, he realizes, "I'm going to get it, man." He is scared. He is shaking; he is screaming. The guards grabbed him. The court, what do they feel? Well, all these people who have had the law violated say, "Wow, that really took something for that judge to do, but at least he respects the law." "I lost someone I loved because of this guy." And now a penalty. They feel safe because the law will be protected. "I can really walk in the streets safely. Someone's going to teach it." But that doesn't help the kid any.

Now they bring in the gas chamber. They're setting it up right there in court. The kid is shaking and screaming. Finally, they lead him over to the gas chamber. And then, deep in the hearts of the people, there is a question, "Maybe the dad doesn't really love his son. We've heard that he did, but maybe he doesn't. Maybe his heart got hard because of all the things that his kid did, and now he really doesn't care whether his son lives or dies." That's the question they have in their minds.

You know what happened? When the door is opened to the gas chamber, the judge comes down off his bench; he takes off his robe; he walks over to his son, and he says, "Son, step aside." And he goes into the gas chamber, and he dies in his son's place.

Now, what does that do to the people? They see that the judge cared so much about his law that he was willing to uphold it.

And what does it do to the son? It shows him that his father loved him. And yet His father loved so much that he would not be sentimental; he would uphold the law.

What did God do?

Jesus came and Jesus died.[39]

---

[39] Winkie Pratney, The Atonement, Agape Force, sound cassette.

REFLECTION AND DISCUSSION

What did God do to help ensure the future good conduct of those guilty of breaking His moral laws?

_____

_____

_____

What are the reasonable conditions for mercy/pardon?

_____

_____

_____

Was Christ's death a literal acceptance of our punishment or an acceptable substitute for our punishment? Why?

_____

_____

_____

Why is having a biblical view of the Atonement so significant?

_____

_____

_____

Chapter Six
Proximity

Proximity: a place or space in which friendship or revolution
occurs, usually when close in distance with someone.
But it is good for me to draw near to God.
PSALM 73:28, NKJV

Recently, my son Dan sent me an article he wrote about a special event in his daughter's life and the spiritual insights he received from that experience. Upon reflection, I began to see the connection between a friendship with God and the concept of proximity.

One Sunday morning, I went to church to witness my eight-year-old daughter being baptized. I remember how excited and nervous she was, leading up to that day. The thought that she would have to stand up in front of the whole church and her family was incredibly thrilling, but daunting. My parents joined us in our church on this special occasion, and as I sat in the front row next to my father, I felt a strong presence from the Lord. As I looked at my dad, I knew he could feel it too. I had sat in church for weeks and had not felt the Lord as strongly as that day.

Maybe it was my daughter being baptized, or it might have been my father next to me: I heard God say, "Proximity." I felt strongly that it was not the traditional sense of being spiritually close to God that made the difference. It was the literal sense that I chose to be as close as I could physically be to His presence. I realized then how closely we are to what is going on physically directly correlates to our spiritual proximity to God.

My son then went on to explain:

Our lives revolve around what we are in proximity to. Are the people in our lives good or bad influences? What are we choosing to read and watch? How are we spending our time, and where? Are we part of a church community that seeks God? Our lives are marked by an intentional effort not just to show up and sit in the back of the classroom, but the front. Not just to go to prayer service, but to engage in it.

There is a massive difference between a football player who is actively part of the play and a teammate sitting on the bench. Both are on the field, but that proximity to the action of events is vital to how the player can affect the game. You cannot just sit on the bench and expect to be the most valuable player on the team. The most valuable players are those who seek out the action and contribute.

In psychology, how close a person is comfortable being to another person physically is often referred to as proxemics. The closer we are physically to someone, the more intimate the relationship. When you talk to your best friend, you stand much closer to them than if you just met someone for the first time. If you had an unpleasant experience with someone, you can't stand being in the same room. This seems obvious when we see it happening to us, but we are often oblivious when we do it to someone else. Especially the Lord.

Finally, Dan shared a challenge for all of us to consider.

How close do you want God to be? Is He at arm's length, or are you actively embracing Him? If He is far away, how can you expect to have an intimate relationship with Him?

Think of a time in your life when you could say you were truly in love. The feeling you get when you are around them, the anguish of being apart, the excitement you get when you learn more about them, and the hope of a return to their presence. Did you desperately want to know and spend more time with them?

For a few years, Leonard Ravenhill was my next-door neighbor. He would say, "Our problem is we don't know God."[40] Is your relationship and proximity to God so close that you can say you "know" God?

Consider your day as an hourglass with twenty-four hours of sand. You will naturally use some for sleeping, eating, working, but how much for God?

When we stuff our time with things that please us, how on earth do we find time to get close to God? If we don't draw close to God, how can we have a standard to set our lives to? If we don't have a standard, then what is right and wrong is entirely up to us. You might say, "Shouldn't God want to see me happy?" What is your definition of happiness? Is it what brings you momentary pleasure or everlasting joy?

There is a famous line in the movie *Braveheart* where Robert the Bruce confronts his father after he betrays William Wallace.

Robert the Bruce: "Those men who bled the ground red at Falkirk, they fought for William Wallace, and he fights for

---

[40] Leonard Ravenhill, "We Don't Know God!," SermonIndex.net, 8 min., 12 sec., https://www.youtube.com/watch?v=zIN49gL7bLQ&ab_channel=SermonIndex.net.

something that I never had. And I took it from him when I betrayed him. I saw it in his face on the battlefield, and it's tearing me apart."

Robert's Father: "All men betray. All lose heart."

Robert the Bruce: "I don't want to lose heart. I want to believe as he does."[41]

Romans 3:23 says, "For all men have sinned and all fall short of the Glory of God." The first step in moving forward is taking ownership and admitting our mistakes. God desperately wants to be in close proximity to us once again. However, we cannot do that without removing those items in our lives that take us away from being in close proximity to Him. This is not a competition of who has sinned the most or has the craziest story. Because of God's glory and grace, it makes no difference how big and heavy our burdens are; they can all be laid down at the foot of the cross.

THE DISCIPLE JESUS LOVED

On four occasions in the book of John, the author refers to himself as "the disciple Jesus loved." I believe this is significant because John was not just claiming to be Jesus' disciple, but that he had a special place in Jesus' heart. I don't know if this is something that Jesus revealed to John or something that he deduced from the way Jesus treated him. In either case, it is quite a claim and something that could give us insight into the issue of proximity.

---

[41] IMDb, "Braveheart Quotes," last modified April 5, 2025, https://www.imdb.com/title/tt0112573/quotes/?item=qt0440113.

John's mother, Salome, asked Jesus if he and his brother could sit on Jesus' right and left in His kingdom. Jesus explained that it was His Father's decision, but He didn't rebuke her for requesting (see Matthew 20:22-23). Some Bible scholars think that Salome and Mary, the mother of Jesus, were sisters. (This would have made John and Jesus first cousins.) Regardless, I believe John's family passionately believed they had to do more than just follow Jesus; they had to get as close as possible to Him.

I don't believe it was an accident that John sat close to Jesus at the Last Supper. I believe he wanted to ensure he heard everything Jesus said. Only John was close enough to hear His whisper. As a result, John discovered who Jesus' betrayer would be. We know that Peter may have had leadership qualities, but he was positioned too far away from Jesus at a critical moment.

When Jesus was crucified, He looked upon the crowd who had gathered. Amazingly, Mary, His mother, was still there with Him. But next to her side was John. By this time, Jesus had seen John's character faithfully displayed on many occasions. John had proven his love for Jesus by trying to be close to Him no matter the cost. Because John, like Mary, always wanted to be near Jesus' side, they were now to be nearer to one another.

ABIDE IN ME

"I am the true vine, and My Father is the vinedresser. Every branch in Me that does not bear fruit He takes away; and every branch that bears fruit He prunes, that it may bear more fruit. You are already clean because of the word which I have spoken to you. Abide in Me, and I in you. As the branch cannot bear fruit of itself, unless it abides in the vine, neither can you, unless you abide in Me" (John 15:1-4, NKJV). The word "abide" is used ten times in the first ten verses of John 15.

Looking at the Greek roots of the word, we discover some helpful definitions. To abide is to "dwell," "remain," "be present," and to "be held and kept." Abiding addresses our posture and place. Later, the Apostle John addresses the issue of sin and gives us the key to overcoming it. "Whoever abides in Him does not sin" (1 John 3:6). We must live in proximity to Him to have the strength to say "no" to sin.

Jesus is not just recommending that we draw closer. He is not presenting abiding as a suggested Christian option. He is stating that our spiritual life depends upon our abiding in Him. Can you get any closer than abiding? God sees the need for connection with us at the deepest level. He won't force Himself on us, but He is waiting for us to respond. Where are we in proximity to Christ?

Years ago, I was challenged by this statement: "You are as close to God as you want to be right now. Time will not change this; it will only reinforce it."

THE POWER OF TOUCH

Proximity makes touch possible. Touch can be experienced both physically and spiritually. Touch matters in the same way that abiding does, and abiding matters the same way that touch does. Thinking about touch, I appreciate these beautiful expressions.

> "Babies who are regularly held and touched gain weight faster, develop stronger immune systems, crawl and walk sooner, sleep more soundly and cry less than babies deprived of close physical contact. Children who are given plenty of physical affection show more task orientated

behavior, less solitary play and less aggression at school. They also achieve higher levels of educational qualifications in later life."[42]

"Physical contact with infants also affects caregivers. Physiologically, physical contact with infants, particularly frontal contact, stimulates the release of oxytocin, which is associated with nurturing behaviors and positive mood . . . Behaviorally, when in close physical contact with infants, caregivers learn more readily to recognize infants' signals—when they are asleep, when they are awake, when they are hungry. Such awareness enhances caregivers' responsiveness to infants."[43]

"What are the long-term deficits that are common in children who are deprived of human touch? Some of these children have developed 'indiscriminate friendliness'—they're more likely to go off with strangers. It's almost as if they think 'all adults are wonderful,' and they don't have the sense 'there are particular adults that are mine.'"[44]

God designed each of us to experience touch. When this occurs spiritually with God, we get stronger, healthier, and wiser spiritually. We also experience deeper sleep and less anxiety. But this touch also affects God. It stirs up His parental affec-

---

[42] "The Power of Touch," *Baby Sensory*, Accessed: April 15, 2025, https://www.babysensory.com.au/power_of_touch.

[43] Ann E Bigelow, Lela Rankin Williams, "To have and to hold: Effects of physical contact on infants and their caregivers," *National Library of Medicine*, September 20, 2020, https://pmc.ncbi.nlm.nih.gov/articles/PMC7502223/.

[44] Katherine Harmon, "How Important is Physical Contact with Your Infant?," *Sci Am*, May 6, 2010, https://www.scientificamerican.com/article/infant-touch/.

tion. It enhances His responsiveness to our needs. Conversely, when we are too far removed from God, we can be led astray by strange voices and forget who we are meant to be with. "And many false prophets will arise and lead many astray" (Matthew 24:11).

I fear that most of us don't yet have the spiritual discernment needed to navigate our culture's many deceptions and distractions. As in the days of Jesus, few of us are so bold (or desperate) as to have the courage to reach out and touch Him.

> "And a woman was there who had been subject to bleeding for twelve years, but no one could heal her. She came up behind him and touched the edge of his cloak, and immediately her bleeding stopped. 'Who touched me?' Jesus asked. When they all denied it, Peter said, 'Master, the people are crowding and pressing against you.' But Jesus said, 'Someone touched me; I know that power has gone out from me.' Then the woman, seeing that she could not go unnoticed, came trembling and fell at his feet. In the presence of all the people, she told why she had touched him and how she had been instantly healed. Then he said to her, 'Daughter, your faith has healed you. Go in peace.'" (Luke 8:43-48)

Her touch released a transfer of power. It made an impact on Jesus as well as herself. Jesus was anxious to meet this stranger who threw caution to the wind for a chance to touch Him. He wanted to get to know her more. When we touch God, we both are affected, often deeply.

FOLLOW THE WHISPER

Consider what God taught the great prophet Elijah about proximity. "The LORD said, 'Go out and stand on the mountain in the presence of the LORD, for the LORD is about to pass by.' Then a great and powerful wind tore the mountains apart and shattered the rocks before the LORD, but the LORD was not in the wind. After the wind there was an earthquake, but the LORD was not in the earthquake. After the earthquake came a fire, but the LORD was not in the fire. And after the fire came **a gentle whisper**. When Elijah heard it, he pulled his cloak over his face and went out and stood at the mouth of the cave" (1 Kings 19:11-13).

This story of Elijah in the cave is fascinating. You might recall, he had just experienced one of the greatest demonstrations of God's power when he successfully challenged the prophets of Baal. God had responded with fire from heaven so everyone could see who the real God was. But that was just the start; Elijah then announced to King Ahab about an impending rainstorm—this was miraculous because the region had experienced drought for three and half years (see 1 Kings 18).

It was a time of revelation and renewal. God was cleansing the nation of its sin and idolatry. A new day had dawned, filled with hope and promise. But there was one problem that remained: Jezebel, the wife of Ahab, remained obstinate and unfazed by the awesome acts of God. She put out a contract on Elijah's life. She was more determined than ever to destroy him and the message he shared with the people.

This is what caused Elijah to seek refuge on Mount Sinai. He went to the place where even the devil couldn't find him. Elijah thought the solution was to run from his problem. This seemed reasonable. However, what awaited him was not.

When Elijah arrived at the cave, God was waiting. Initially, God spoke to Elijah like He spoke to the people who had hardened their hearts and followed other gods. This show of power and authority was effective in getting Elijah's attention.

However, Elijah needed something more than power: he needed connection. As strange as it might seem, Elijah needed a change of proximity to God. He needed a closer connection to God. I believe that is why God often whispers.

Could God be whispering to you today? Could you, like Elijah, be facing a choice and a challenge to draw near to His mystery, His holiness, His tenderness?

When Elijah made his way to the mouth of the cave, he instinctively did something that reflects our typical response. The Scripture said he "pulled his cloak over his face." To me, this indicates shame or fear. How many times have these mindsets come in the way of a closer proximity to God? Let's explore this through the lens of author Eugene Kennedy.

> Friendship is the tiny whispering sound after the earthquake and fire, the soft invitation that brought the prophet Elijah out of the cave in which he had taken shelter. Relationship—that much-abused word—is not a whirlwind but a soft breeze; when we hear it, we can give up the shelter of our own selfishness and discover life. It is profoundly ironical that those who seek to master life by being number one, by winning above all else, often seem hurt and confused—and desperately lonely—when the mighty noise of their self-centeredness turns into a hollow echo. Yet those who see friendship as the path to life are faced with liking themselves aside for the sake of others, to give up wanting to be number one.[45]

How do we move closer? The Bible says that initially, God draws us to Himself. "No one can come to me unless the Father who sent me draws them" (John 6:44). However, after the

---

[45] Kennedy, *On Being a Friend,* 76, 77.

initial encounter, He waits for us to take the initiative. The Bible encourages us to "Come close to God, and God will come close to you" (James 4:8).

Many Christians lack experiencing a deeper level of friendship with God. Why? It might be because they are currently too passive—God always responds to those who intentionally move closer.

LOVE MAKES A WAY

Christians often bemoan that they haven't spent sufficient time praying or reading the Bible. When I hear this, for some reason, I keep thinking back to when I was dating in high school and spent close to two hours talking to my girlfriend on one particular night. During that call, I wasn't thinking, "When will she stop talking and let me move on to better things?" On the contrary, it didn't matter what else I needed to do that day; this was my priority. Talking to her was the most important activity in my life at the time.

Why? Because love makes a way.

If we struggle to take time with God, it is likely because our heart's desire for Him has experienced a slow fade. He is no longer the apple of our eye, the treasure buried in the field, or the pearl of great price. Something has dimmed His glory and perfection. Something has distracted us.

If you find yourself wondering why God feels so far away, remember, He has made a way. Jesus made a way for you to run to the Father. You can run to God when you feel like it, and you will find Him. You can run to God when you don't feel like it, and you will find him. Be disciplined. Be loving. Run to God; He made the way.

HINDERANCES TO PROXIMITY
LACK OF TIME

I believe one of the most uncomfortable subjects to come up in a discipleship class is the subject of personal prayer. If we polled how many Christians are satisfied with their prayer lives, how many would say, "Yes"? Throughout my walk with the Lord, I have battled this feeling of regret and disappointment regarding my prayer life.

One of my problems is that I love to read biographies of the saints of old, and I judge myself through the lens of their relationship with God. Many of them had incredible prayer lives. They got up hours before dawn. They prayed outside in the winter until the snow melted around them. Grooves were discovered on the wooden floors where their knees made constant contact in prayer.

One day, the Lord gave me insight and hope; He said, "I don't want you to look at prayer as an activity or event. I want you to treat it as a lifestyle." This opened up the world to me. Smith Wigglesworth once said, "I don't often spend more than half an hour in prayer at one time, but I never go more than half an hour without praying." I am now more focused on living like He is always there with me, no matter what I am doing. He is never far from my thoughts, and I am never far from His side.

OFFENSES

Sometimes we ask God for help and experience a delay. Nobody likes to wait, and oftentimes we get frustrated with Him and the process. On other occasions, we experience some form of criticism, neglect, or abuse from others. This, too, like being forced to wait, can lead to questioning God's love for us.

When we unfairly suspect Him of indifference, we start to reciprocate in our worship and service to Him. We may give God some of our heart, but not all of it.

Furthermore, we may have experienced past hurts with our earthly father or stepfather. In response, we may have learned not to trust fathers or men or even seek to have a meaningful relationship. Either way, because there has been a breakdown in trust, there may also be a fear of intimacy with others, and, more importantly, God.

THE ENEMY

To become God's friend, we must stop seeking to be a friend of this world. This is not negotiable and never changes with God. His word is clear: "Don't you realize that friendship with the world makes you an enemy of God? I say it again: If you want to be a friend of the world, you make yourself an enemy of God" (James 4:4, NLT). This issue of trying to simultaneously be loved by this world and loved by God has caused many believers to become stuck in their journey of friendship.

Whenever we try to deepen our relationship with God, the devil will try to distract us and make it as difficult as possible to have an open channel with Him. It seems like the devil is constantly giving false information on God's character and motives. It is common to face a flood of random thoughts that confuse and rob us of spiritual contentment. The Bible is clear in how we should respond: "Submit yourselves, then, to God. Resist the devil, and he will flee from you" (James 4:7). When we submit ourselves completely, God gives the power to resist him.

Many Christians face dark nights of the soul when a veil or cloud separates them from sensing God's love. These are the times of testing when we must hold onto God's promises and trust in His character. The Bible tells us what David did in these trying circumstances. "Now David was greatly distressed, for the people spoke of stoning him, because the soul of all the people was grieved, every man for his sons and his daughters. But David strengthened himself in the LORD his God" (1 Samuel 30:6, NKJV). This is where true faith is forged.

LACK OF REST

A few years ago, I had a heart attack. It caused a change in my thinking: I cannot always go full speed. The fact that I still have some partially blocked arteries is a reminder that I will have to watch my pace for the rest of my life. There are historical cases where horses kept running, under the direction of a rider, until they died. They were called warhorses. God hasn't called us to be warhorses.

Jesus would often take time to be alone with His Father. Sometimes, He would leave the crowds and fellowship only with His disciples. He knew that constant sacrifices would cease to be a joy if there was no time for recuperation.

Without hesitation, I can say that I have loved my fifty-three years of full-time ministry. I can also say that there were times that I couldn't function effectively. Several times, I admitted to my coworkers and family that I was operating at an unsustainable pace. Those were times I had to pause and listen for His voice. And in my fatigue, I sensed Jesus' whisper: "Come to me, all you who are weary and burdened, and I will give you rest. Take my yoke upon you and learn from me, for I am gentle and humble in heart, and you will find rest for your souls. For my yoke is easy and my burden is light" (Matthew 11:28-30).

WHAT FRIENDS DO

"Soulmate" has been defined as a close friend or romantic partner with whom one has a unique, deep connection based on mutual understanding and acceptance. Much has been said about the deep friendship David had with Jonathan. Not to take away from their friendship, but David's friendship with God was even greater.

David was king of Israel but saw God as the King of kings. Not only that, but David also considered God to be his close and personal friend. In turn, God referred to David as "A man after God's own heart" (1 Samuel 13:14). This mutual love and respect led David to consider increasing God's honor among the people. This was an uncommon viewpoint. The more common perspective of the people of Israel was found in the book of Haggai. "'You expected much, but see, it turned out to be little. What you brought home, I blew away. Why?' declares the LORD Almighty. 'Because of my house, which remains a ruin, while each of you is busy with your own house'" (Haggai 1:9).

One day, David came up with an idea that would honor God, his friend. "He said to Nathan the prophet, 'Here I am, living in a house of cedar, while the ark of God remains in a tent.' Nathan replied to the king, 'Whatever you have in mind, go ahead and do it, for the LORD is with you.'" (2 Samuel 7:2-3).

David's desire to honor God by building Him a temple brought an immediate response from God. "Your royal house will remain in my presence forever. Your throne will be established forever" (2 Samuel 7:16).

This promise from God then caused David to respond back,

"'Who am I, Almighty LORD,' he asked, 'and why is my house so important that you have brought me this far? And even this you consider to be a small act, Almighty LORD. You've also spoken about the distant future of my house. Almighty LORD, this is the teaching about the man. What more can I, David, say to you, Almighty LORD, since you know me so well! You've done this great thing because of your promise and your own desire. You made it known to me. That is why you are great, LORD God. There is no one like you, and there is no other god except you, as we have heard with our own ears.'"
(2 Samuel 7:18-22)

I would encourage you to read the entire chapter of 2 Samuel 7. It is a beautiful exchange of two individuals focused on honoring the other. It is a beautiful example of what happens when we determine to be God's friend.

DRAW ME NEARER

Fanny Crosby

I am Thine, O Lord, I have heard Thy voice,
And it told Thy love to me;
But I long to rise in the arms of faith,
And be closer drawn to Thee.

Refrain:
Draw me nearer, nearer, nearer, blessed Lord,
To the cross where Thou has died;
Draw me nearer, nearer, nearer, blessed Lord,
To Thy precious bleeding side.

Consecrate me now to Thy service, Lord,
By the pow'r of grace divine;
Let my soul look up with a steadfast hope,
And my will be lost in Thine. [Refrain]

Oh, the pure delight of a single hour
That before Thy throne I spend,
When I kneel in prayer, and with Thee, my God,
I commune as friend with friend! [Refrain]

There are depths of love that I cannot know
Till I cross the narrow sea;
There are heights of joy that I may not reach
Till I rest in peace with Thee. [Refrain][46]

---

[46] Hymnary.org, "Draw Me Nearer," last modified April 15, 2025, https://hymnary.org/text/i_am_thine_o_lord_i_have_heard_thy_voice.

REFLECTION AND DISCUSSION

What would a prayer lifestyle be like for you?

_____

_____

_____

Name some of the things that may be keeping you from being in close proximity to the Lord.

_____

_____

_____

Give an example of when God personally touched your life.

_____

_____

_____

How could you honor God more with your life?

_____

_____

_____

Chapter Seven
Friendship is the Crown

"To the Ancients, Friendship seemed the happiest and most fully human of all loves; the crown of life and the school of virtue."
C.S. LEWIS[47]

And when the Chief Shepherd appears, you will receive the crown of glory that will never fade away.
1 PETER 5:4

A LESSON FROM 9/11

Of all the stories that came out of 9/11, this one is probably the most memorable for me.

On September 11, 2001, Cantor Fitzgerald, a top global financial services firm, suffered a devastating loss when 658 employees perished in the World Trade Center attacks. CEO Howard Lutnick, who survived because he was taking his child to school that morning, was heartbroken by the tragedy.

Determined to support the victims' families, Lutnick pledged 25% of the firm's profits for five years and donated

---

[47] Goodreads, "C.S. Lewis," last modified April 15, 2025, https://www.goodreads.com/quotes/1399706-to-the-ancients-friendship-seemed-the-happiest-and-most-fully.

$180 million to them. He also offered jobs to their children, securing their future in a time of immense loss. By 2016, 57 of those children had joined Cantor Fitzgerald, keeping their parents' legacy alive.[48]

This story of resilience, generosity, and corporate responsibility continues to inspire, showing the power of compassion and leadership in times of crisis.

Over the years, I have contemplated what activities and character qualities deepen my friendship with God. I've discovered quite a few. In this chapter, I want to submit key points to help you have a deeper friendship with God.

MY FRIEND IS THE KING

In 95 A.D., the Apostle John was exiled to the Greek island of Patmos on the Aegean Sea. He may have been deprived of country and friends, but he still found solace with his greatest friend. But on a particular Lord's Day, he heard a loud voice behind him. Suddenly, John was confronted with the glorified Christ. His response was immediate: "When I saw him, I fell at his feet as though dead. Then he placed his right hand on me and said: 'Do not be afraid. I am the First and the Last'" (Revelation 1:17). The best position for friendship with God is a bended knee and humble heart. This was the position the Apostle John took the day he received a clear and dramatic revelation of Jesus.

John had been given a glimpse of the glorified side of Jesus on the Mount of Transfiguration, but this was much more

---

[48] Lucila Aguada, *About Resilience*, November 3, 2022, https://www. aboutresilience.com/committing-to-culture-of-goodwill-cantor-fitzgerald-on-9-11/.

personal. He was reminded that his friend was also the King of kings and the Lord of lords. John had experienced a key to intimacy. "The Lord is a friend to those who fear him" (Proverbs 25:14, NLT). Without this, sin will soon be crouching at our door. It is sin which breaks the bonds of friendship with God. And we have all experienced what that feels like.

As John bowed in reverential awe, Jesus responded with a touch of compassion. The glorified Son of God reminded John that He is also gentle and kind.

Francis Chan frames the beauty of God's character: "I doubt there are hardly any of us that grew up with fathers who were strong authorities and also intimate with us. It is hard to understand how you could have both in one being. I've tried my whole life to be that kind of dad to my kids. That I'm strong; I'm the leader of my home but you're my best friend and you know I would do anything for you."[49]

RAW HONESTY

I remember reading a story of a woman's supernatural healing. She had pleaded with God over several months and even years. Frustrated with a lack of progress, she was so upset with the situation that she swore at God before passing out from the pain. Ironically, when she awoke, she was healed.

Since reading that unusual story, I have made it a point to be more honest with God. I don't swear, but I articulate my honest feelings to Him. In every case, I received a positive response from God. Often, it is comforting and encouraging.

---

[49] Francis Chan, "I'm Leaving in 2020 'Be Fishers of Men,'" BRMinistries, 27 min., 34 sec., https://www.youtube.com/watch?v=bnxdk9SZUqw& ab_channel=BRMinistries.

I've been given such assurance of His love. To know that He loves me even when I'm a mess, makes such a difference in my outlook. His presence changes everything. Even as I write this, I'm crying because He is again showing me how much He loves me (and us). He longs to hold us in His arms. He promises to never leave or forsake us.

In our sorrow, it is much better to share our honest selves with God instead of trying to impress Him with our religious speech and efforts. After the death of their brother Lazareth, Mary and Martha shared their sorrow with Jesus; His response was tears. Their honesty moved His heart in an amazing way. Alexander MacLaren's comments on this key principle:

> "If we are friends of God, we shall have no secrets from Him. There are very few of those who are dearest to us to whom we could venture to lay bare all the depths of our hearts…. Tell God all, if you mean to be a friend of His. And do not be afraid to tell Him your harsh thoughts of Him, and your complaints of Him. He never resents anything that a man who loves Him says about Him, if he says it to Him. What He resents—if I might use the word—is our huddling up grudges and murmurings and questionings in our own hearts, and saying never a word to the friend against whom they offend. Out with it all, brethren! Complaints, regrets, questionings, petitions, hot wishes, take them all to Him; and be sure that instead of their breaking, they will, if spoken, cement the friendship which is disturbed by secrecy on our parts."[50]

---

[50] Alexander MacLaren, "MacLaren's Expositions of Holy Scripture – James 2," *Bible Hub*, Accessed April 15, 2025, https://biblehub.com/commentaries/maclaren/james/2.htm.

I believe this is what drew Ruth the Moabite to Naomi and Naomi's God. She saw Naomi could complain honestly about God and not fear condemnation (see Ruth 1:20-21). She also saw that the God of the Israelites had displayed compassion by coming to the aid of His people (see Ruth 1:6). Ruth was drawn to the nature and character of the God of the Bible. She, like Naomi, could share honestly with Him.

ATTENTIVE LISTENING

I grew up in a small community in northern Minnesota. Our neighborhood had many children who were close to my age. When I sought permission to go and play with my friends, my mother would admonish me, "Okay, but don't stray beyond the sound of my voice. Lunch will be ready soon." Simple but powerful words. If we could only position our lives in such a way that we never drift beyond the sound of His voice. This would give us the ability to immediately respond to Him whenever He calls.

A year ago, my wife said that I needed to go to the ear doctor and get my hearing checked. She apparently was having to repeat herself too often when speaking to me. Well, I went in for the first time in my life. Fortunately, it was a painless experience. When they had completed all the tests, they began to tabulate the results. The doctor finally came in and said, "You were normal across the wide sound spectrum—except one particular frequency." Curiously, I asked what that frequency was, and she replied, "That frequency is the sound of a woman's voice!"

I have to admit that it made me smile. Perhaps I had more of an excuse for not responding to my wife's voice—probably not. Since then, I have needed to look more at her face when she speaks. It also helps to turn down any other sounds that may drown out her voice.

I bring this up to highlight an important spiritual truth. Many people have become dull to God's voice. They need to focus more on listening and turn down the other competing voices. It is not an issue of convenience; it is an issue of survival.

Dan Rather, the famous CBS anchor, once asked Mother Teresa what she said during her prayers. She answered, "I listen." So, Dan turned the question and asked, "Well then, what does God say?" Mother Teresa smiled with confidence and answered, "He listens." For an instant, Dan didn't know what to say. "And if you don't understand that," Mother Teresa added, "I can't explain it to you."[51]

Certainly, there are times when it is appropriate to cry out to the Lord. But let's not forget to "be still and know that I am God" (Psalm 46:10). If you truly desire to be a friend of God, both sides must listen. One of the greatest prophets in the Bible was Samuel. His lengthy ministry began at an early age, when he simply said to God, "Speak Lord for your servant heareth." I want that to be my heart posture always.

Our ministry once opened a coffee shop in a dangerous neighborhood in the inner core of Minneapolis. Most of our patrons were hardcore heroin addicts. Growing up in a small community, I wondered if I had the experience necessary to help them. After facing numerous trials and failures, I remember hearing a wise admonition, "They don't care what you know until they know that you care." To me, that meant changing my focus from talking to listening.

---

[51] Darren Ethier, "Just Listening," *Sermon Central*, May 9, 2002, https://sermoncentral.com/sermon-illustrations/sermon-illustrations-about-just?keyword=Just.

Later, I served as a chaplain for our county's sheriff's department. My first call to a death notification was very memorable. The woman had lost her husband and was very distraught. To help her, I shared some thoughts and suggestions. She immediately rebuffed them. Momentarily, I felt rejected, but then realized I was focusing more on pithy suggestions than compassionate listening. She needed heartfelt empathy more than heartless advice.

Another example was when I worked as a chaplain at a faith-based treatment center. Every day was filled with one-on-one counseling sessions with clients. Initially, I was tempted to share my knowledge and steps to stay sober on a sustained basis. However, I soon discovered that I lacked the connection necessary to impact their lives. That only changed when I prioritized listening over speaking. I stopped interrupting them to get a point across. If they interrupted me, I would immediately stop talking. Ever since then, I have tried to practice this in all my conversations.

HEART TO HEART

I have learned that, generally, God speaks from His heart to our hearts. This way, He can convey His feelings as well as His thoughts. I believe this is a more effective form of communication. So, how can we identify God's voice? In most cases, God leads our hearts with His heart. This is the opposite of the enemy. The devil pushes and makes demands in our minds without any comfort or love.

God leads, often by small and simple insights. It reminds me of the prophet Elijah. The Scriptures tell us Elijah was supernaturally fed by birds. How much food can a bird carry? Not very much. Fortunately, there are many birds so collectively it adds up. I found that God gives us supernatural insights a "bird's portion" at a time. Perhaps to not overwhelm us. Perhaps to make us savor every morsel.

Several years ago, I began to journal what He would say to my heart. Most often, it would be a few words or a couple of sentences. I did this so that I wouldn't forget exactly what He had said. God's voice is like a butterfly. If you don't catch it quickly, it will soon be lost.

Since I began, I discovered another good reason for journaling; I wanted God to know that I would cherish and apply whatever He shared. My hope is that it will encourage Him to share even more. Eventually, that journal grew to several hundred entries. One day, the Lord told me to write a book. Not knowing where to begin, He prompted me to use my journal as the basis of my first book, *Consuming Love*.

The last benefit of journaling is based on something a missionary said many years ago: "Seek to become a voice, not an echo." This has challenged me to seek God daily for fresh insights into His Word and a keen sensitivity to His voice in prayer. If I do this, I will often have something fresh and relevant for others. I believe that was the way Jesus lived. "When Jesus had finished saying these things, the crowds were amazed at his teaching, because he taught as one who had authority, and not as their teachers of the law" (Matthew 7:28-29).

MUTUAL TRUST

I want to say something a bit controversial: Don't seek God's love; you already have that. Seek His trust. That's the challenge.

The Apostle John was the only disciple who was clearly present at Jesus' crucifixion. This reflected John's ongoing commitment to Jesus. As a result, Jesus trusted him so much that He entrusted the care of his mother to John. "When Jesus therefore saw His mother, and the disciple whom He loved standing by, He said to His mother, 'Woman, behold your son!' Then He said to the disciple, 'Behold your mother!' And from that hour that disciple took her to his own home" (John 19:26-27). Jesus loved all His disciples the same, but He didn't trust them all equally. Jesus' trust in John was far different than His trust in Judas Iscariot.

A coworker said something years ago that I never forgot. He said the Lord spoke to him and said, "I trust you to trust me." Perhaps God can't trust us until we've learned to trust Him. Our coins have declared "In God we trust," but can God trust us? Alexander MacLaren stated that mutual trust and confidence are "the very lifeblood of friendship. You cannot say someone is your friend, but do not trust him."[52] Furthermore, "Unless I trust God I cannot be a friend of God's. If you and I are His friends we trust Him, and He will trust us . . . So that, if I trust God, I may be sure that God trusts me, and, in His confidence, leaves a great deal to me; and so ennobles and glorifies me by His reliance upon me."[53]

The book of Job is a fascinating story. Many can relate to Job's trials and test of faith. Although suffering abounds throughout the story, it does have a happy conclusion. Job is healed and restored. In fact, his life becomes even better. When everything is said and done, we can easily forget what started it all. The devil claimed that Job only served God because He blessed Him. If the blessings stopped, then Job would stop serving the Lord. That was the claim that turned into a

---

[52] Kennedy, *On Being a Friend*, 18.

[53] Alexander MacLaren, "MacLaren's Expositions of Holy Scripture – James 2," *Bible Hub*, Accessed April 15, 2025, https://biblehub.com/commentaries/maclaren/james/2.htm.

challenge. God stopped blessing Job and allowed the devil to torment him to prove that Job was trustworthy. The story is about trust. God trusted Job, and Job proved Him right.

The story of Job should prompt us to consider how much God trusts us. What if the devil wanted to challenge our commitment to God? Would God be as confident in us as He was with Job?

FAITHFULNESS

Faithfulness is the basis for trust. God earns our trust through His faithfulness more than His love. Have we earned His trust through our faithfulness to Him? Can others trust us? Have we earned their trust by our faithfulness? If you are willing to compromise your faithfulness, it demonstrates you do not value it.

When the Bible is clear about God's design for sex, and then we disregard or violate that plan, what does that say to God? If we don't know God, that's one thing. But if we are trying to establish a friendship built on love and trust, and then we blatantly violate His will and desires, what are we saying? Doesn't it question the sincerity of our hearts? When it comes to friendship, don't our actions speak louder than our words? Our position on moral issues is not established in a vacuum. God will always be affected by our choices, especially if our goal is to be His friend.

Integrity is revealed, not in the big stuff, but the small stuff. Most people don't rob banks and perform acts of terrorism. People are much more willing to compromise their integrity on the little stuff, and when they are alone. It could be a lie, cheating on a test, or visiting a porn site. Remember, heaven is tracking everything we do. How are we known in heaven?

LOOSE LIPS SINK SHIPS

One time, the Lord spoke to me and said that there were certain things He only shares with His friends. What a challenging statement! There have been several times in my life when I thought that God had blessed me to the point of embarrassment. In those moments, I hesitate to tell all He has done because I fear others will compare themselves and feel overlooked. I also need to guard my heart from the subtle sin of pride.

King Hezekiah made a strategic blunder when he showed the Babylonians all his royal treasures. In his effort to impress them, he inadvertently invited them to steal the blessings God had given him. God's secrets are sacred treasures, and we must not use them to gain likes and views. It could come back to hurt us.

Have you noticed that Jesus didn't advertise His miracles? Often when someone was healed, He would ask them to keep quiet. Unfortunately, the people were anxious to let the world know what happened. The Apostle Paul seemed to convey a similar attitude. When he needed to convey a personal experience, he intentionally avoided drawing attention to himself (see 2 Corinthians 12:2-4). Friends are careful not to dishonor what was meant to be a private personal experience.

Naturally, friends treat each other differently from other people. For one thing, they can tell each other secrets because they trust each other. They feel that their secrets are safe with the other person.

HUMILITY AND RESPECT

There is another aspect to this friendship with God that is critical. Friends wouldn't consciously say or do things that would hurt their friend. They would naturally avoid that which dishonors them. They wouldn't argue that it is too hard. They would recognize it as acceptable practice amongst friends. It is a price that is not unreasonable or too high.

If we desire to be God's friend, then we will not consciously do things that hurt Him. We will avoid the things that bring Him pain. We will be careful not to offend and disrespect Him, especially publicly. The Ten Commandments remind us: "You shall not take the name of the LORD your God in vain, for the LORD will not hold *him* guiltless who takes His name in vain" (Exodus 20:7, NKJV).

I remember preparing for a ministry conference. I was responsible for putting together a media presentation of older members of our organization. To do so, I was able to collect numerous childhood and teen photos of these people. One picture caught my attention. It was a certain staff member when he was a teen. During that time, he had battled severe acne. I thought, "Wow, this photo will shock people." As I was weaving it into the presentation, that person came by and saw what I was doing, and said, "Please, don't show that picture." In my immaturity and insensitivity, I did it anyway. It got a reaction from the crowd that I suspected. But I hurt someone whom I respect as a leader and a friend. This was a person who was godly and kind. But knowing that should have caused me to be careful not to dishonor him.

But what would you think if I posted this picture on social media or in this book? Wouldn't that bring additional hurt to my friend? What if I attached to the picture his full name and address? Wouldn't that also be disrespectful and cruel? If I valued our friendship, I would stop doing things that would hurt him. So, it is with God. Rather than finding peace with our sin, we must stop doing things that would damage our friendship.

When confronted with our sin, we often think of the negative consequences to ourselves. Many encourage us not to be so hard on ourselves. But what if we adopted God's perspective? What if we saw our sin in the context of hurting God and damaging our friendship?

A woman shared with me an incident that happened in her first year of marriage. Several men began to harass her publicly. They made degrading, spiteful comments that broke her heart. But that wasn't the worst part. They said all of this in the presence of her husband. Tragically, her husband failed to defend or support her. Eventually, that marriage fell apart because she no longer trusted or respected her husband.

A wise Christian leader said the greatest danger in the Western Church is leaders possessing too much personal ambition. The disciples certainly suffered from it. "Then Peter chimed in, 'We left everything and followed you. What do we get out of it?'" (Matthew 19:27, MSG). I confess that I have been guilty of the same. Using God to advance our own personal ambitions is one of the most disrespectful things we can do to Him.

THE LOYALTY OF LOVE

There is a special loyalty wrapped up in every true friendship. The Bible gives us some beautiful examples of this: "But Ruth replied, 'Don't urge me to leave you or to turn back from you. Where you go I will go, and where you stay I will stay. Your people will be my people and your God my God. Where you die I will die, and there I will be buried. May the LORD deal with me, be it ever so severely, if even death separates you and me'" (Ruth 1:16-17).

Ruth's attitude towards her mother-in-law, Naomi, was similar to Ittai's attitude towards King David. "But Ittai replied to the king, 'As surely as the LORD lives, and as my lord the king lives, wherever my lord the king may be, whether it means life or death, there will your servant be'" (2 Samuel 15:21). Both Ruth and Ittai had a level of commitment that transcended all the uncertainties and dangers that would come with their relationship. They sacrificed their personal ambitions and comforts for the sake of someone they highly esteemed.

Finally, we see this tenacious loyalty with Elisha and his master, Elijah. Three times Elisha stated, "As surely as the LORD lives and as you live, I will not leave you" (see 2 Kings 2:1-6). Elisha's commitment to Elijah yielded great spiritual rewards. I believe this is the loyalty that God is looking for. God has given it first to us. Now He waits for us to return it to Him.

JOYFUL SURRENDER

Friends are interested in what pleases their friends. They will often take an interest in these things because their friend is interested. Likewise, we should "carefully determine what pleases the Lord" (Ephesians 5:10).

Jack Deere once said, "Preachers/teachers are often giving people something to do instead of a person to enjoy. There is a huge difference between serving someone because we have to and serving someone we enjoy. What is a friend of God?

Someone who enjoys God. It is more than service. There is a special chemistry with them."[54]

There are numerous passages of Scripture that encourage us to delight in our friendship with God. "Was not our ancestor Abraham considered righteous for what he did when he offered his son Isaac on the altar? You see that his faith and his actions were working together, and his faith was made complete by what he did. And the scripture was fulfilled that says, 'Abraham believed God, and it was credited to him as righteousness,' and he was called God's friend" (James 2:21-24).

God's friendship with humans has often been marveled at. Alexander MacLaren says of this relationship,

> "Abraham's gift of his son to God was but a feeble shadow of God's gift of His Son to men. And if the surrender on the part of the human friend was the infallible token of his love, surely the surrender on the part of the heavenly Friend is no less the infallible sign of His love to all the world. Generalize these thoughts and they come to this. If we are God's lovers, God will give us Himself, in so far as we can receive Him; and all other gifts in so far as they are good and needful. If we are God's friends and lovers we shall give Him, in glad surrender, our whole selves . . . Yield yourselves to God, and in the giving of yourselves to Him, you will get back yourselves glorified and blessed by the gift. There is no friendship if self shuts out the friend from participation in what is the

---

[54] Dr. Jack Deere, "Friendship with God," Antioch Baton Rouge, 42 min., 18 sec., https://www.youtube.com/watch?v=02DVzHJdpH0&ab_channel=AntiochBatonRouge.

other's."[55]

FRIENDLY PERSUASION

The Bible says that God shares His secrets with His prophets (see Amos 3:7-8). His prophets knew God in a more intimate way than most. When you look at the story of Sodom and Gomorrah, you find that God was not willing to give the go-ahead on judgment until He talked with Abraham. Some describe it as divine consultation. Abraham was His friend, and God knew the decision would greatly affect Abraham and his family.

Another example was Moses. There was a time when God had determined to destroy the Israelites because of their consistent rebellion (see Numbers 14). However, God decided not to do so until He was able to share with Moses and get his perspective on the matter. Moses presented another possibility that involved sparing the people of Israel. Surprisingly, God deferred to Moses' suggestion because of the friendship they had.

These biblical accounts should give us a deeper appreciation for prayer. God is anxious to hear the perspective of His friends. He values their insights and will take them into account on a host of matters. Phillips Brooks once said, "Prayer is not conquering God's reluctance, but taking hold of God's willingness."[56]

---

[55] Alexander MacLaren, "MacLaren's Expositions of Holy Scripture – James 2," *Bible Hub,* Accessed April 15, 2025, https://biblehub.com/commentaries/maclaren/james/2.htm.

[56] Acts 413 Ministries, "Quotes on Prayer," Accessed May 27, 2025, https://www.acts413.net/quotes

FROM DUTY TO DESIRE

There is a Bible principle that is particularly important: knowledge equals responsibility. You see this illustrated throughout Scripture, from Adam and Eve to the Children of Israel, to the early Church. God will judge us based on the spiritual understanding we possess. For example, God will consider the actions of a young child differently than an adult. He will judge a person who lived in a remote tribal village differently than someone who grew up in a Christian home in America. The Bible says, "Will not the Judge of all the earth do right?" (Genesis 18:25).

Some would complain that it would be better not to increase their knowledge of God and His ways to avoid increased accountability. To those individuals, I would remind them that to know God is to love Him. Our deeper understanding of Him only increases our love. The more we love, the more we shift from duty to desire. To live to please a friend is much more sustainable than to serve someone only out of duty. On this matter, MacLaren offers this delightful perspective:

> "All the slavery of abject submission, of reluctant service, is clean swept away, when we understand that friendship and love find their supreme delight in discovering and in executing the will of the beloved. And surely if you and I are the friends of God, the cold words, 'duty,' 'must,' 'should,' will be struck out of our vocabulary and will be replaced by 'delight,' 'cannot but; will.' For friends find the very life—[57]—of their friendship in mutual obedience."

---

[57] Alexander MacLaren, "MacLaren Expositions of Holy Scripture - James 2," *Bible Hub*, Accessed April 15, 2025, https://biblehub.com/commentaries/maclaren/james/2.htm.

Many have asked me, "Are there levels in heaven and hell?" Based on this principle of knowledge equals responsibility, we could assume that. I have come across a scripture that suggests this very thought. "Women received back their dead, raised to life again. There were others who were tortured, refusing to be released so that they might gain an even better resurrection" (Hebrews 11:35). The passage suggests our sacrifice for the Lord has rewards in heaven. Could that reward be closer to Him in eternity?

We all have heard of "golden crowns" in heaven. The imagery paints a beautiful picture. But while the idea of golden crowns might fill us with wonder, let's not forget heaven has streets paved with gold. Gold probably doesn't have the same value in heaven that it does on earth. One day, thinking of the reality of God's eternal kindness and rewards for those He loves, a new phrase dropped into my spirit: "Friendship is the crown." Now, that is something that just might be more valuable than gold, and a crown that we can wear even now.

JUST A CLOSER WALK WITH THEE

I am weak, but Thou art strong;
Jesus, keep me from all wrong;
I'll be satisfied as long
As I walk, let me walk close to Thee.

Refrain:
Just a closer walk with Thee,
Grant it, Jesus, is my plea,
Daily walking close to Thee,
Let it be, dear Lord, let it be.
Through this world of toil and snares,
If I falter, Lord, who cares?
Who with me my burden shares?
None but Thee, dear Lord, none but Thee. [Refrain]

When my feeble life is o'er,
Time for me will be no more;
Guide me gently, safely o'er
To Thy kingdom shore, to Thy shore. [Refrain][58]

---

[58] Hymnary.org, "Just a Closer Walk with Thee," last modified April 16, 2025, https://hymnary.org/text/i_am_weak_but_thou_art_strong.

REFLECTION AND DISCUSSION

How would you describe a healthy fear of the Lord?

_____

_____

_____

Do you practice listening to God? How do you hold on to the insights that He gives you?

_____

_____

_____

How much do you think God trusts you?

_____

_____

_____

Give suggestions on how we can demonstrate humility and respect for God and others.

_____

_____

_____

Chapter Eight
Feed My Sheep

"The only way to have a friend is to be one."
RALPH WALDO EMERSON[59]

Jesus said, Feed my sheep.
JOHN 21:17

A DRAMA OF THE DARK

One of the world's most renowned women is Helen Keller, a prodigy who lived and became famous without access to sight or sound. But Helen Keller had another self, another half, if you will.

Anne Sullivan was born in Feeding Hills, Massachusetts. During her childhood, an illness left her partially blind. Her mother died, her dad abandoned her, and she lived her remaining childhood years in institutions for orphans. Under the care of the state, she endured unsuccessful surgeries to heal her eyes. But then, at the Perkins Institute for the Blind, a brilliant operation restored her sight. Sullivan, thereafter, devoted herself to the care of the blind.

---

[59] Brainy Quote, "Ralph Waldo Emerson Quotes," last modified April 15, 2025, https://www.brainyquote.com/quotes/ralph_waldo_emerson_100740.

Meanwhile, in Tuscumbia, Alabama, Helen Keller was re-covering from her own illness, though she would never hear or speak again. By the grace of God, Helen Keller came under the care of Anne Sullivan. Anne taught her thirty words in only two weeks, spelling them by touching her hand. Under Sullivan's care, Helen Keller learned, graduated from college, and became a prolific author and activist. For forty-nine years, the two were inseparable.

A time came when misfortune befell Anne Sullivan. What misfortune? She became blind. And now, Helen devotedly taught her to overcome the lack of sight.

Standing at Anne's deathbed, when it was all over, she said, "I pray for strength to endure the silent dark until she smiles upon me again."[60]

THE CALL TO FRIENDSHIP

Recently I heard my wife's frustrated voice coming from the bathroom. She had just struggled to get the hairdryer to work, and now she seemed to be struggling with another bathroom appliance. At the time, I was deeply immersed in a Bible study in my office. My inward thoughts were something like, "What now? Can't Martha see I'm trying to write a book about friendship with God?" Fortunately, it only took a moment before I caught the irony of it all. How could I love the One I could not see if I could not love the one I could see? As we pursue a sacred quest to become God's friend, we eventually come to this conclusion: You can't be a friend of God's unless

---

[60] Roland Ledoux, "Death of Helen Keller's Tutor," *Oasis Bible Ministry*, January 6, 2023, https://forgodslove52.com/2023/01/06/death-of-hellen-kellers-tutor/.

you learn to be a friend to others. Loving others is God's heart and it must be ours as well.

MODEL OF FRIENDSHIP

Why do you think children were drawn to Jesus? Because He was safe and engaging. He was friendly. This morning, I read a fascinating interchange with Jesus and the children.

> "Jesus entered the temple courts and drove out all who were buying and selling there. He overturned the tables of the money changers and the benches of those selling doves. 'It is written,' he said to them, 'My house will be called a house of prayer, but you are making it "a den of robbers."' The blind and the lame came to him at the temple, and he healed them. But when the chief priests and the teachers of the law saw the wonderful things he did and the children shouting in the temple courts, 'Hosanna to the Son of David,' they were indignant. 'Do you hear what these children are saying?' they asked him. 'Yes,' replied Jesus, 'have you never read, "From the lips of children and infants you, Lord, have called forth your praise?"'" (Matthew 21:12-16)

Did you catch it? I had never noticed it before. Even with Jesus' indignation over the moneychangers, the children were unfazed in their love and respect for Him.

Why were sinners drawn to Jesus? Because He didn't distance Himself from them. He was friendly. "The Son of Man came eating and drinking, and they say, 'Here is a glutton and a drunkard, a friend of tax collectors and sinners'" (Matthew 11:19).

Although most religious leaders hated Him, Jesus ministered privately to a Pharisee named Nicodemus. What makes the God of the Bible so unique among other religious gods? He is friendly. Not just Jesus but the entire Godhead. Jesus said, "Anyone who has seen me has seen the Father" (John 14:9). Jesus sought out the lost sheep. The Spirit comforts us in times of need. The Father ran to his prodigal son. That's what friends do.

WASHING FEET

One day, I was driving home alone from the treatment center where I served as a chaplain. I love listening to Scriptures while in my car. On this day, I was listening to the book of John, specifically the thirteenth chapter. Suddenly, without realizing my actions, I cried out loudly, "No!" These are the words I heard that day:

> "Jesus knew that the Father had put all things under his power, and that he had come from God and was returning to God; so he got up from the meal, took off his outer clothing, and wrapped a towel around his waist. After that, he poured water into a basin and began to wash his disciples' feet, drying them with the towel that was wrapped around him.
>
> "He came to Simon Peter, who said to him, 'Lord, are you going to wash my feet?'
>
> Jesus replied, 'You do not realize now what I am doing, but later you will understand.'
>
> 'No,' said Peter, 'you shall never wash my feet.'
>
> Jesus answered, 'Unless I wash you, you have no part with me.'
>
> 'Then, Lord,' Simon Peter replied, 'not just my feet but my hands and my head as well!'"
> (John 13:3-9)

I had heard and read this story many times before but, on this day, the Holy Spirit brought it to life. I felt like Peter, who didn't want the King of kings to serve him in such a humiliating way. No, God, this is too much. Please don't bend your knee for my sake! Please don't hold my dirty, stinking feet tenderly in your hands. It's enough that you came and taught us the way; You don't have to demonstrate what we need to do. You are God, and we are but blades of grass that quickly wither in the wind (see Psalm 103:15-16).

I believe that outside of the crucifixion, Jesus' most significant act of love was washing the disciples' feet. In this world, it is typical for the most famous to be the most pampered and privileged. Unfortunately, this has carried over to some Christian leaders and musical artists. Jesus' life was the opposite. At the pinnacle of His popularity and influence, He was humble and selfless. Jesus was the greatest servant of all, not by proclamation but by demonstration.

If that wasn't enough, what Jesus said after washing His disciples' feet was equally amazing. "When he had finished washing their feet, he put on his clothes and returned to his place. 'Do you understand what I have done for you?' he asked them. 'You call me "Teacher" and "Lord," and rightly so, for that is what I am. Now that I, your Lord and Teacher, have washed your feet, you also should wash one another's feet. I have set you an example that you should do as I have done for you. Very truly I tell you, no servant is greater than his master, nor is a messenger greater than the one who sent him'" (John 13:12-16).

What is Christ's message to us? Put others first. As God blesses you, don't get proud or demanding. How can we be His friend if we do not join Him in this? Most of Christ's followers will not become rich or famous. However, we all can serve others in His name.

God has called us to serve and not in a way that would reflect quickly in our favor. The Apostle Paul exhorted the early church to "be content with obscurity, like Christ" (Colossians 3:3-4, MSG). What is a test of friendship with God? When we are content to serve others in secret.

THE SPIRIT OF GENEROSITY

In the book of Acts, we find an interesting development. Shortly after the disciples were baptized by the Holy Spirit (see Acts 2), they began to display a change in behavior. "All the believers were together and had everything in common. They sold property and possessions to give to anyone who had need. Every day they continued to meet together in the temple courts. They broke bread in their homes and ate together with glad and sincere hearts" (Acts 2:44-46). A sign of the disciples' encounter with God appeared to be an extraordinary spirit of generosity towards others. This generosity was demonstrated in the sharing of resources as well as the sharing of their time.

This was further displayed when they had a second encounter with the Holy Spirit. The Bible states that the power of God shook the place where they were praying. After this, "All the believers were one in heart and mind. No one claimed that any of their possessions was their own, but they shared everything they had" (Acts 4:32).

In this context, we are given the sad story of Ananias and Sapphira (see Acts 5:1-11). Yes, there was judgment because they lied to the Holy Spirit. But there was more going on. Ananias and Sapphira had chosen to resist the spirit of generosity God had poured out upon them and their friends.

They projected themselves as friends of God while rejecting the revealed heart of God. Let us be encouraged to action by these words from Eugene Kennedy:

> "Friendship and love are successful in proportion to our willingness to break the boundaries of our own self-absorption. We achieve the vitality of free relationships with others only as we die to our own selves to make room for others in our lives. The secret that is no secret about friendship resides in self-forgetfulness, in living for others rather than just ourselves."[61]

EYES ON THE MASTER

Recently, I took a trip out west with my wife, Martha. I was able to visit the Grand Canyon for the first time. It was something I have always wanted to do, and I was finally able to check it off my bucket list. The weather was perfect, and the Grand Canyon was certainly majestic and beautiful. I surmised that no painting or photo could do it justice. The sight of a canyon 227 miles long, up to eighteen miles wide, and one mile deep is simply overwhelming. It reminded me of the greatness and beauty of God.

But there was something else I witnessed shortly after our visit to the Grand Canyon that was also inspiring. Martha and I found ourselves travelling peacefully down a small country road when a tractor suddenly pulled out in front of us and then stopped in the middle of the road. My immediate reaction was, "That's a bit rude." After bringing our vehicle to an abrupt stop, I realized the rancher was intently trying to get a herd of sheep across the road. It was then I saw what the rancher was looking

---

[61] Kennedy, *On Being a Friend*, 126.

at. It wasn't the sheep in the road or the cars that were stopped. He was looking at only one thing, his sheep dog.

Up to that point, I hadn't noticed the dog, but now I was getting the picture. I quickly turned my attention to the sheep dog and noticed how intently he was looking at his master. With a few short commands, the dog directed the final wayward sheep safely across the road. To this day, I cannot get the intensity of the sheep dog's gaze on his master out of my mind. He was so alert, smart, and ready to obey the slightest command of his master. I was deeply impressed.

As I continued past the scene, I reflected on Jesus being the Good Shephard. However, this time, I didn't see Him alone with His sheep. Now there was a loyal helper with Him. Someone who hung on every word and gesture He would give. This helper wanted nothing more than to please His master.

I recall being invited to preach at a church some time ago; as I waited near the front to be introduced to the congregation, I heard in my spirit, "Lead them to greener pastures." I believe this is our mandate as Christians whether we hold a formal leadership position or not. However, it cannot be accomplished outside of the context of following the Good Shepherd. So, I have to ask myself, "Am I a good sheep dog? Do I intentionally live to please the wishes of my Master? Will I help Him lead His sheep to greener pastures?" I certainly hope so. The Grand Canyon was magnificent to me, but to be God's loyal sheep dog, is magnificent to Him.

A RUDE AWAKENING

Shortly after giving my life to Christ, I attended the Discipleship Training Institute in Fresno, California. The ten-week program provided a solid foundation for my faith. I grew more spiritually during that time than at any other time. It was like a spiritual greenhouse filled with powerful teachers and students hungry to know more about God.

I shared a room with five other guys. We became fast friends, and I am in touch with some of them fifty years later. But there was one guy that I didn't connect with as easily. I will call him Bob. For some reason, I didn't think he was as hungry for God as the others were. I didn't have any deep spiritual discussions with him and doubted if he was making as much progress as the others.

About halfway through the program, we all had a change of rooms. Everyone was given a new set of roommates. Initially, I felt bad because I had gotten to know everyone but Bob. When the new roommates were announced, to my shock, Bob was one of my new roommates. No one knew my thoughts about Bob, but he was in my room again for the rest of the training.

When graduation came, we all cried and wished each other the best. I can't remember if I said anything to Bob, but I was confident I would not see him again. In my mind, he didn't have the spiritual pedigree or drive for God to use him. He seemed satisfied with a mediocre relationship with God. He was content in being a good neighbor.

Fast forward forty years.

I got an invitation to go to a church picnic in my home state of Minnesota. This church had been incredibly supportive of me and my family over the years. It had a wonderful pastor and plenty of great Christian families. I decided it would be an honor to go.

Shortly after I arrived, someone told me that Bob was there. I was utterly shocked because I didn't know he had ever attended this church. After all these years, would he even remember me? So, I walked up and introduced myself; sure enough, he remembered. And then I asked him what he had been doing for the last forty years.

He had been a missionary for years in Africa. He had planted many churches, held evangelistic meetings where many had been saved, healed, and delivered. God had used him to make an enormous impact in a needy part of the world.

Mic drop.

As he showed me pictures and shared stories, I slipped further down in my seat. How could I have been so wrong?

I believe God purposely puts a "Bob" in all our lives. Have you noticed that whether it is in school, at work, or in the neighborhood, there is always someone we don't naturally connect with. I used to think it was their problem, but now I believe otherwise. God is in the process of perfecting our love while He is perfecting His love in others. It reminds me of Jesus' admonition to His followers:

> "You're familiar with the old written law, 'Love your friend,' and its unwritten companion, 'Hate your enemy.' I'm challenging that. I'm telling you to love your enemies. Let them bring out the best in you, not the worst. When someone gives you a hard time, respond with the supple moves of prayer, for then you are working out of your true selves, your God-created selves. This is what God does. He gives his best—the sun to warm and the rain to nourish—to everyone, regardless: the good and bad, the nice and nasty. If all you do is love the lovable, do you expect a bonus? Anybody can do that. If you simply say hello to those who greet you, do you expect a medal? Any run-of-the-mill sinner does that. In a word, what I'm saying is, 'Grow up.' You're kingdom subjects. Now

live like it. Live out your God-created identity. Live
generously and graciously toward others, the way God
lives toward you."
(Matthew 5:43-48, MSG)

PREPARE FOR ARRIVAL!

Another parable cluster is found in Matthew 24 and 25. This
time, Jesus was talking to His disciples about the Last Days.
After telling them the signs to look for, He shared three parables
about preparing for His return:

1. A master gave his servant supervisory responsibilities
    but didn't tell him when he would return. He said if this
    servant focused on benefiting others, he would be wise
    and faithful. However, if the master came home to find
    the servant neglecting or harming the other servants, he
    would be considered wicked and be severely punished.

2. Ten virgins were involved in a wedding event. They all
    brought oil lamps to light the way for the bridegroom's
    symbolic journey to the bride's house. Unfortunately,
    the bridegroom was a long time coming, and as a result,
    all ten women fell asleep. When the bridegroom finally
    arrived, five women realized they didn't have enough oil
    to keep their lamps burning. In a frantic effort to buy
    more oil, they missed their opportunity to attend the
    wedding banquet.

3. A master planned an extended trip, gave money to three
    of his servants, and charged them with stewarding the
    money as best as they could. When the master returned,
    those who neglected investing their money were
    criticized and punished. Those who invested their
    money were rewarded with additional talents.

A central theme of the three parables is the importance of vigilance regarding Christ's return. Again, this was important because of Jesus' audience. He was instructing His twelve disciples, who were expected to carry on His mission. Jesus was concerned they would get distracted, careless, or slothful in fulfilling their calling. Like John the Baptist, they needed to "prepare the way for the Lord" (see Mark 1:2-3).

THE SHEEP AND THE GOATS

But there was another point Jesus wanted to make that was equally important to spiritual alertness. Jesus wanted to clearly identify where their focus should be. He wanted them to know where God's heart was. To answer that, Jesus shared a final parable regarding God's Final Judgment:

> "When the Son of Man comes in his glory, and all the angels with him, he will sit on his glorious throne. All the nations will be gathered before him, and he will separate the people one from another as a shepherd separates the sheep from the goats. He will put the sheep on his right and the goats on his left.
>
> "Then the King will say to those on his right, 'Come, you who are blessed by my Father; take your inheritance, the kingdom prepared for you since the creation of the world. For I was hungry and you gave me something to eat, I was thirsty and you gave me something to drink, I was a stranger and you invited me in, I needed clothes and you clothed me, I was sick and you looked after me, I was in prison and you came to visit me.'
>
> "Then the righteous will answer him, 'Lord, when did we see you hungry and feed you, or thirsty and give you something to drink? When did we see you a stranger

and invite you in, or needing clothes and clothe you? When did we see you sick or in prison and go to visit you?'

"The King will reply, 'Truly I tell you, whatever you did for one of the least of these brothers and sisters of mine, you did for me.'

"Then he will say to those on his left, 'Depart from me, you who are cursed, into the eternal fire prepared for the devil and his angels. For I was hungry and you gave me nothing to eat, I was thirsty and you gave me nothing to drink, I was a stranger and you did not invite me in, I needed clothes and you did not clothe me, I was sick and in prison and you did not look after me.'

"They also will answer, 'Lord, when did we see you hungry or thirsty or a stranger or needing clothes or sick or in prison, and did not help you?'

"He will reply, 'Truly I tell you, whatever you did not do for one of the least of these, you did not do for me.' Then they will go away to eternal punishment, but the righteous to eternal life."
(Matthew 25:31-45)

These four parables reveal the importance of focusing on being a friend to others until Christ's return. This is a critical point. Those who do this as a lifestyle will not be found lacking, even if Christ comes back unexpectedly. Countless Christians would like to be regarded as God's friend. However, it is clear in Scripture that friendship with God is contingent upon our faithfully caring for others. This divides good servants from evil ones; it separates wise and foolish virgins; and ultimately, it divides the sheep from the goats.

I SHALL NOT PASS AGAIN THIS WAY

W.R. Fitch

The bread that bringeth strength I want to give;
The water pure that bids the thirsty live.
I want to help the failing, day by day.
I'm sure I shall not pass again this way.

I want to give the oil of joy for tears,
The faith to conquer crowding doubts and fears;
Beauty for ashes may I give away.
I'm sure I shall not pass again this way.

I want to give good measure running o'er,
And into angry heart I want to pour
The answer soft that turneth wrath away.
I'm sure I shall not pass again this way.

I want to give to others hope and faith;
I want to do all that the Master saith;
I want to live aright from day to day.
I'm sure I shall not pass again this way.[62]

---

[62] Hymnary.org, "I Shall Not Pass This Way Again," last modified April 15, 2025, https://hymnary.org/text/the_bread_that_giveth_bringeth_strength_.

REFLECTION AND DISCUSSION

Compare the Church today with the one described in the book of Acts.

_____

_____

_____

How can we demonstrate the friendliness of Jesus?

_____

_____

_____

What qualities of a sheep dog could we exhibit in following the Good Shepherd?

_____

_____

_____

Have you ever struggled in loving certain people? How did you handle the situation? How do you think Jesus would treat them?

_____

_____

_____

Chapter Nine
Come as Servants, Leave as Friends

"A rule I have had for years is: to treat the Lord Jesus Christ as a personal friend. He is not a creed, a mere empty doctrine; but it is He Himself we have."
D. L. MOODY[63]

I will do what you have asked, because I am your friend and I am pleased with you.
EXODUS 33:17, CEV

REUNION TO REMEMBER

The invitation for an Agape Force reunion immediately created anxiety. I knew I should go, but I didn't know how the experience would be. I decided to ask my son to accompany me. We would have a long road trip to talk and enjoy some quality time together. And the potential would be that Dan would experience something special that would help him in his spiritual journey.

When we arrived in Texas, I was taken aback by all the loud, exuberant conversations. People seemed to be genuinely thrilled

---

[63] Brainy Quote, "Dwight L. Moody Quotes," last modified April 15, 2025, https://www.brainyquote.com/quotes/dwight_l_moody_157629.

to see old friends and fellow workers. Again, I thought about my son seeing so many elderly people being so loud and excited. Would he be turned off or drawn into their excitement?

At one point, as I was observing all the activity, I sensed the Lord say, "Come in as servants, leave as friends." It reminded me of the words of Jesus during the Last Supper. I realized that John 15:15 was not some historical record of Christ's interaction with His disciples but a blueprint of the Christian life. God intends that all of us begin as servants but finish as friends. This is not only true with Him but with each other.

As Dan and I continue to fellowship, worship, and share meals with our fellow reunioners, this truth became even more real in my spirit. By the end of the three-day reunion, there was such unity, love, and transparency that I felt as if we were experiencing heaven on earth. Although many years had passed and some names forgotten, this was a reuniting of spirit that brought us closer than ever. Now, months later, I can't think about the experience without my heart melting. Tears well up quickly when I consider this, and I will treasure the memory of it for the rest of my life.

HE KNOWS MY NAME!

It is astonishing and humbling to consider how carefully God has followed our lives. He is the Good Shepherd, and He knows not only His flock, but every sheep personally and intimately.

"Now Mary stood outside the tomb crying. As she wept, she bent over to look into the tomb and saw two angels in white, seated where Jesus' body had been, one at the head and the other at the foot.

"They asked her, 'Woman, why are you crying?'

"'They have taken my Lord away,' she said, 'and I don't know where they have put him.' At this, she turned around and saw Jesus standing there, but she did not realize that it was Jesus.

"He asked her, 'Woman, why are you crying? Who is it you are looking for?'

Thinking he was the gardener, she said, 'Sir, if you have carried him away, tell me where you have put him, and I will get him.'

"Jesus said to her, 'Mary.'

"She turned toward him and cried out in Aramaic, 'Rabboni!'"
(John 20:11-16)

Notice the state that Mary Magdalene was in initially. She was not only traumatized by the loss of the love of her life, but she also thought His grave had been robbed. She couldn't imagine who or why anyone would do such a deplorable, hurtful, evil deed. Her suffering was immeasurable. Desperate for answers, she asked anyone who could help, even a stranger. Shocked and amazed, she heard the most comforting word in the world.

She heard her name.

Not only that, but it was spoken by the love of her life—Jesus. With that, her countenance, perspective, and life improved dramatically. This is what a close friend does. Amid our suffering, they come and address us personally and lovingly. And when our suffering comes from a misunderstanding of them, they come with reassurance of their faithfulness.

FRIENDSHIP BRINGS HOPE!

No matter how difficult life is, there is always hope when God is involved. If we are His friends, He has already yielded the option of noninvolvement. "God is not a man, that He should lie, Nor a son of man, that He should repent. Has He said, and will He not do? Or has He spoken, and will He not make it good?" (Numbers 23:19, NKJV). I like how author Terence E. Fretheim puts this self-limitation by God:

> "As in any relationship of integrity, God will have to give up some things for the sake of relationship. Thus, God will have to give up some freedom. Any commitment or promise within a relationship entails a limitation of freedom. By such actions, God has decisively limited the options God has for speaking and acting. God has exercised divine freedom in the making of such promises in the first place. But, in having freely made such promises, thereafter God's freedom is truly limited by those promises. God will do what God says God will do; God will be faithful to God's own promises, and that is a limitation of freedom. God's freedom is now most supremely a freedom for the world, not a freedom from the world.
>
> Moreover, any relationship of integrity will entail a sharing of power. Each party to the relationship must give up any monopoly on power for the sake of relationship. Neither party to the relationship can be overwhelmed for the relationship to be a true one. For the sake of the relationship, God gives up the exercise of some power. This will in turn qualify any talk about di-

vine control or divine sovereignty. Total control of the other in a relationship is no relationship of integrity."[64]

This is the friendship that will sustain us when life becomes difficult, and we face constant fear and danger. "You are my friend, my fortress, where I am safe. You are my shield, and you made me the ruler of our people" (Psalm 144:2, CEV).

This is what King David experienced, and it is there for us. "You, LORD, were my friend, and you made me strong as a mighty mountain" (Psalm 30:7, CEV).

When we understand God's commitment to a relationship of integrity, then we can hold fast to hope and overcome the fear that seeks to control our lives!

FRIENDSHIP BRINGS REVELATION

At the Last Supper, Jesus explained to His disciples what was to come. He said, "Before long, the world will not see me anymore, but you will see me" (John 14:19). So, who did Jesus appear to after His resurrection? Was it Caiaphas the high priest, or other members of the Sanhedrin? Was it Pontius Pilate or the Roman soldiers? Was it the unsaved masses who cried, "Crucify Him, Crucify Him"? No, not one of them.

If I were Jesus, I would have been very tempted to appear before my enemies. I would have wanted to rub their noses in it. I would have tried to put the fear of God in them. I would want them to shrivel in shock and regret that they ever attacked me. But Jesus was never vindictive or proud. He carefully chose who to bless with His presence. He chose His friends.

---

[64] Terence E. Fretheim, *The Suffering of God* (Fortress Press, 1984), 36-37.

I am confident that after Jesus was crucified, the religious leaders thought it would be a simple cleanup operation. The Pharisee Gamaliel reinforced their sentiments by pointing out that previous insurrections ended because the leader was killed. However, what he and the religious leaders didn't know was that the disciples' leader was not dead.

When Jesus rose from the dead, He appeared to His friends. He appeared to His disciples (see John 20:19-21, 21:1-14; Luke 24:13-35). He also appeared to Mary Magdalene, as previously mentioned. Finally, He appeared to the apostles. "And we apostles are witnesses of all he did throughout Judea and in Jerusalem. They put him to death by hanging him on a cross, but God raised him to life on the third day. Then God allowed him to appear, not to the general public, but to us whom God had chosen in advance to be his witnesses. We were those who ate and drank with him after he rose from the dead" (Acts 10:39-41, NLT).

FRIENDSHIP BRINGS PARTNERSHIP

From the beginning, God intended to partner with us. We were never meant to be servants only. Friends naturally like to do things together, "For we are God's fellow workers" (1 Corinthians 3:9, NKJV).

Adam was not just formed from the dust of the earth, but God gave him a job description—he was tasked with being the caretaker of the Garden of Eden.

A few years ago, I felt God leading my wife and me to purchase a house in central Minnesota. From the moment I walked in, I had the sense that this was God's house, but He was allowing me to be its caretaker. I have always enjoyed that perspective. When Jesus was challenged to pay the temple tax, He resolved the problem by partnering with His friend Peter. As a result, they were both taken care of (see Matthew 17:24-27). Jesus was always including His friends in His activities. St Augustine once said, "Without God, we cannot; without us, God will not."[65] That's how it works.

It may seem rather simple, but while praying on the altar a while back, I sensed God say to me, "We've been through a lot together." This simple statement has melted my heart. More recently, my daughter shared a dream she had about me. She said that I was standing with Jesus on a hill overlooking a valley. Jesus simply said, "That was quite the journey, Steve." These images are encouraging because they tell me that I have never been alone. He was with me in dark places as well as glorious light. It has been a journey together marked by tragedy and victory. Through it all, I've discovered the deepest recesses of His heart.

The beauty of God's friendship is that it will never end. Other friends come and go, but He has always been there and always will be.

Can I be honest with you? I am totally in love with God and always will be. He has been my perfect friend.

---

[65] Quotefancy, last modified April 15, 2025, https://quotefancy.com/quote/905675/Saint-Augustine-Without-God-we-cannot-Without-us-God-will-not.

FRIENDSHIP BRINGS PROTECTION

Job faced incredible trials and tribulations. There were times when he struggled to maintain an unoffended heart. After his encounter with God, something unusual happened. God stood in staunch support of Job in the face of his "so-called" friends:

> "After GOD had finished addressing Job, he turned to Eliphaz the Temanite and said, 'I've had it with you and your two friends. I'm fed up! You haven't been honest either with me or about me—not the way my friend Job has. So here's what you must do. Take seven bulls and seven rams, and go to my friend Job. Sacrifice a burnt offering on your own behalf. My friend Job will pray for you, and I will accept his prayer. He will ask me not to treat you as you deserve for talking nonsense about me, and for not being honest with me, as he has.'" (Job 42:7-8, MSG)

There was a time when Moses' brother and sister decided to challenge his leadership. God's response was quick and to the point:

> "At once the LORD said to Moses, Aaron and Miriam, 'Come out to the tent of meeting, all three of you.' So the three of them went out. Then the LORD came down in a pillar of cloud; he stood at the entrance to the tent and summoned Aaron and Miriam. When the two of them stepped forward, he said, 'Listen to my words: "When there is a prophet among you, I, the LORD, reveal myself to them in visions, I speak to them in dreams. But this is not true of my servant Moses; he is faithful in all my house. With him I speak face to face, clearly and

not in riddles; he sees the form of the LORD. Why then were you not afraid to speak against my servant Moses?'" The anger of the LORD burned against them, and he left them." (Exodus 12:4-9)

It is clear in Scripture; God stands up for His friends.

No author is generally connected to Psalm 91, but Jewish tradition believes it was Moses. Listen to God's response to His friend, "'Because he loves me,' says the LORD, 'I will rescue him; I will protect him, for he acknowledges my name. He will call on me, and I will answer him; I will be with him in trouble, I will deliver him and honor him. With long life I will satisfy him and show him my salvation'" (Psalm 91:14-16).

God made those words so real to me one night, and they continue to be a source of strength and hope. God has convinced me that He will never leave or forsake me, no matter the circumstances. No matter how I feel. No matter what others may think.

THE GOOD FOUNDATION

Please allow me to ask an unusual question. What is the foundation of the Kingdom of God, or what is the primary attribute of God? Many would say that it is love.

Seems reasonable, but I have discovered that we will never understand the love of God until we first understand the holiness of God. Holiness was emphasized in the Old Testament, while love was emphasized in the New Testament. Holiness cries out for justice while love cries out for mercy. This led me to believe that the foundation of the Kingdom of God was the combination of two-character qualities—holiness and love.

Recently, however, I have considered that another attribute of God is primary, and it might surprise you. I believe God's goodness is the foundation of His Kingdom. Goodness is quite possibly the most important attribute of God.

When God formed the earth and all of creation, He remarked that it was *very good*. When God made humans, He intended for us to reflect Himself. The Psalmist David said, "Surely your goodness and unfailing love will pursue me all the days of my life, and I will live in the house of the LORD forever" (Psalm 23:6 NLT). This wasn't just a passage about physical blessings. It was a declaration of God's intent to pursue us with the deepest core of His being so that we could reflect His goodness.

MY GOODNESS!

One of the greatest compliments a wife could give about her husband would be, "He has been good to me," or "He's a good man." Moses was one of those good guys. On one hand, he had to lead people who were often rebellious, complaining, and lacking in any spiritual understanding. But on the other hand, he was experiencing God in an incredibly deep and personal way. The Bible says, "The LORD would speak to Moses face to face, as one speaks to a friend" (Exodus 33:11). Moses was confident enough in his friendship with God to speak openly and honestly:

> "Moses said to the LORD, 'I know that you have told me to lead these people to the land you promised them. But you have not said who will go along to help me. You have said that you are my friend and that you are pleased with me. If this is true, let me know what your plans are,

then I can obey and continue to please you. And don't forget that you have chosen this nation to be your own.' The LORD said, 'I will go with you and give you peace.' Then Moses replied, 'If you aren't going with us, please don't make us leave this place. But if you do go with us, everyone will know that you are pleased with your people and with me. That way, we will be different from the rest of the people on earth.' **So the LORD told him, 'I will do what you have asked, because I am your friend** and I am pleased with you.'" (Exodus 33:12-17, CEV)

This exchange clearly reveals the friendship they enjoyed and led Moses to ask God to show him His glory. I find God's response surprising: "And the LORD said, 'I will cause all **my goodness** to pass in front of you, and I will proclaim my name, the LORD, in your presence. I will have mercy on whom I will have mercy, and I will have compassion on whom I will have compassion'" (Exodus 33:19). I find it interesting that God listened to Moses' request and discerned his heart. From that, God determined the best thing for Moses to see was His goodness. It was not God's holiness or even His love. It was His goodness.

So, what is the goodness of God? "God's goodness represents everything that God is, everything that God has and everything that God desires for us to experience. The word 'goodness' in the Hebrew means 'good in the widest sense' of the word. One could say that God is good to the furthest extreme. This God kind of goodness far surpasses anything that the world has to offer."[66]

---

[66] Pastor George, "The Goodness of God," *Eagle Mountain International Church*, December 20, 2022, https://www.emic.org/blog/the-goodness-of-god/#:~:text=%E2%80%9Cgood%20in%20the%20widest%20sense,and%20his%20tender%20mercies%20are.

It is worthwhile to again acknowledge that in the Old Testament, we see an emphasis on the holiness of God. In the New Testament, we see an emphasis on the love of God. His goodness embraces both. If we were to recall the discussion on justice and mercy; goodness honors both. It is accepting without enabling, loving without compromising, trusting yet verifying. It is summed up beautifully in Micah 6:8, "He has shown you, O man, what *is* **good**; And what does the LORD require of you But to do **justly**, To love **mercy**, And to walk humbly with your God?"

I have become impressed with the numerous scriptures that speak of God's goodness:

- "I remain confident of this: I will see the goodness of the LORD in the land of the living." (Psalm 27:13)
- "The earth is full of the goodness of the LORD." (Psalm 33:5, NKJV)
- "For He satisfies the longing soul, And fills the hungry soul with goodness." (Psalm 107:9, NKJV)
- "Or do you despise the riches of His goodness, forbearance, and longsuffering, not knowing that the goodness of God leads you to repentance?" (Romans 2:4)
- "Therefore consider the goodness and severity of God: on those who fell, severity; but toward you, goodness, if you continue in His goodness." (Romans 11:22, NKJV)

True friendship with God will reflect an alignment of heart and mind. This is what will impact the world. The world may tire of the Gospel being preached but it will never tire of the Gospel being lived. We must reflect His goodness in the deepest and truest sense of the word. There is no other way.

COME CLOSER

At my age, I am more focused on finishing well because I know the finish line is not far ahead.

I want to join the Apostle Paul in declaring, "I have fought the good fight, I have finished the race, I have kept the faith. Now there is in store for me the crown of righteousness, which the Lord, the righteous Judge, will award to me on that day— and not only to me, but also to all who have longed for his appearing" (2 Timothy 4:7-8). In my remaining years, I want to focus on finishing the work God gave me over fifty years ago. The greatest honor I could receive on my tombstone would be an epitaph stating, "Friend of God."

Years ago, I had an experience with God that I have never forgotten. I've shared it before, but I believe it is a fitting end to this book.

I saw myself going to heaven and was immediately greeted by loved ones who had passed on before me. While we were rejoicing, a trumpet sounded, and a stately angel walked up to me and said, "The King would have an audience with you." This created some apprehension, but my family and friends encouraged me to follow him.

We walked in this glorious city for some time until we finally reached a building with two massive doors. They opened on their own, and the angel motioned for me to step in. As I did, the doors shut behind me, and I found myself straining to adjust to the lower light.

As I did, I recognized I was in a huge room with someone seated on a throne on the far side. At that point, my knees buckled. I was afraid to move. I felt vulnerable and insecure.

Suddenly, something happened that I didn't expect. I heard a voice say, "Come." I immediately recognized it as the same voice I had heard numerous times on Earth. It was an assuring voice filled with comfort and protection. It was the voice I heard years ago saying, "I want friends!"

Impulsively, I started running to that all-familiar voice. As I reached the steps of His throne, I cast all decorum aside and jumped onto His lap. He immediately laughed, and so did I. We talked as two old friends reuniting. I remember thinking, "He's not spending time with me because that is part of His responsibilities when a new one arrives. He is doing this because it is what He has been waiting to do. His desire for eternal friendship with me was finally realized.

Today, as I reflect on this story—and the meaning of it—I am reminded of God's promise to His friends: "His lord said to him, 'Well done, good and faithful servant; you have been faithful over a few things, I will make you ruler over many things. Enter into the joy of your lord'" (Matthew 25:23, NKJV).

The great revivalist, Jonathan Edwards, once said, "Let it be [our] first love to enter into an everlasting friendship with Christ that never shall be broken."[67]

Amen, Lord Jesus, come.

---

[67] Drew Hunter, "What a Friend We Have in Jesus," *Desiring God*, December 11, 2018, https://www.desiringgod.org/articles/what-a-friend-we-have-in-jesus.

WHAT A FRIEND WE HAVE IN JESUS

Joseph Medlicott Scriven

All our sins and griefs to bear!
What a privilege to carry
Everything to God in prayer!
O what peace we often forfeit,
O what needless pain we bear,
All because we do not carry
Everything to God in prayer!

Have we trials and temptations?
Is there trouble anywhere?
We should never be discouraged,
Take it to the Lord in prayer.
Can we find a friend so faithful
Who will all our sorrows share?
Jesus knows our every weakness,
Take it to the Lord in prayer.

Are we weak and heavy-laden,
Cumbered with a load of care?
Precious Savior, still our refuge—
Take it to the Lord in prayer;
Do thy friends despise, forsake thee?
Take it to the Lord in prayer;
In His arms He'll take and shield thee,
Thou wilt find a solace there.[68]

---

[68] Hymnary.org, "What a Friend We Have in Jesus," last modified April 15, 2015, https://hymnary.org/text/what_a_friend_we_have_in_jesus_all_our_s.

REFLECTION AND DISCUSSION

To whom did Jesus appear to after His resurrection? Why?

_____

_____

_____

Explain some of the benefits of a friendship with God.

_____

_____

_____

What is the foundation of the Kingdom of God?

_____

_____

_____

Explain the goodness of God? How is it connected to friendship?

_____

_____

_____

Acknowledgements

Dan Harrison for his writing skills and spiritual wisdom.

Joshua Harrison for his keen insights and assistance.

Sheryl Thornberg for her talents in cover design. You never cease to amaze me.

Marcus Costantino for his skill in editing. You made the manuscript so much better.

Dave Sheets for providing a wonderful team to work on this project. Once again, you have delivered.

About the Author

Steve Harrison has been an incurable revivalist for over fifty years. Saved during the Jesus Revolution and caught up in a Mexican revival in the mid '90s, he has been forever ruined by God—in a good way. He and his wife, Martha, live in the Brainerd Lakes Area of Minnesota, where they often host their growing grandchildren. Steve continues to serve the Body of Christ as a scribe of God's heart.

For More Information

Steve Harrison
c/o Bethany Urban Development
P.O. Box 320
Brainerd, MN 56401
Phone: 612-598-3270
budministries@gmail.com

Also by Steve Harrison

Consuming Love, Liberating Love, Suffering Love, Clash of Kingdoms, and Restoring the Beauty

Available today from Ardor Media
https://kingsroadministries.com/

Ardor Media
P.O. Box 302
Brainerd, MN 56401

Ardor Media is a division of Bethany Urban Development, a ministry dedicated to promoting transforming revivals in urban communities.

www.ingramcontent.com/pod-product-compliance
Lightning Source LLC
Chambersburg PA
CBHW021638120626
46545CB00002B/606